P9-DEY-140

THE
MILES
BETWEEN
ME

ESSAYS

TONI
NEALIE

CURBSIDE SPLENDOR PUBLISHING

All rights reserved. No part of this book may be reproduced in any form or by any electronic or mechanical means, including information storage and retrieval systems, without permission in writing from the publisher, except in the case of short passages quoted in reviews.

Published by Curbside Splendor Publishing, Inc., Chicago, Illinois in 2016.

First Edition
Copyright © 2016 by Toni Nealie
Library of Congress Control Number: 2015948129

ISBN 978-1940430782
Cover images © Toni Nealie
Author photo © Bruce Sheridan
Design by Alban Fischer
Edited by Naomi Huffman and Catherine Eves

Manufactured in the United States of America.

WWW.CURBSIDESPLENDOR.COM

FOR MY FAMILY

To Dama

Happy
writing, and
reading!

Toni 2016

CONTENTS

UNRAVELING

TRAILING

"We possess nothing in the world—a mere chance can strip us of everything—except the power to say 'I'"
—SIMONE WEIL

I LIKE TO fly. Space and time dissipate with the vapor trail. Bubble-wrapped solitude, headphones, and a book. Deliciously detached. One weekend I flew from Chicago to London to celebrate a family wedding. Eight hours without commitment. The weightlessness of traveling in silvery air, floating without my mother-wife carapace.

The pilot announced our flight path "across" to London. I've always thought of going "up" to London, after flying so many times there from my native land, Aotearoa, New Zealand. Why do we still call the South Pacific down and Europe up? On a globe, a mapmaker positions north and south, but Earth's spin renders arbitrary these irrefutable points. Ancients knew better than to settle into the simplicity of up and down: the Roman goddess Fortuna, "she who revolves around the year," rattled mortals on her wheel of providence. Knowing that today's luck could be tomorrow's fall kept humans aware of life's mutability.

My own life flipped topsy-turvy when I moved from the Southern Hemisphere to America in 2001. My personal coordinates seemed knocked off-kilter, the solid self I thought I possessed became unformed. For a while I cleaved to London as kind of a nest. My eldest sister and her family lived there, my only family in this hemisphere.

I'd spent three years living there in my twenties and had visited many times since. London's muted pigeon-gray light, its drizzle, and pink brick became familiar beauty. So it became "across," a half-way house, until slowly, imperceptibly, incrementally, Chicago became "home," and I transferred my allegiance to wide pavements, big blue skies, yellow and red brick.

On the plane, as it creaked and swayed up through the cumuli, a loud voice sliced through my thoughts. "Hey, I'm Lisa." A willowy woman in yoga pants folded herself into an improbable lotus position on the seat next to me. She thrust out a hand. "Are you on business or pleasure?" Taking her hand, I removed my headphones. Lisa's husband had a job in London and wanted to explore Europe for a few years. She was joining him for a two-week reconnoiter of the city. Should she move there? The blue skies of Colorado versus grey clouds. Giving up her jobs: child psychologist and yoga teacher. All those years of education—for what? Uncertainty, an unfamiliar culture. What should she do?

It posed a dilemma for her, as it had for me. As it *still* does for me, years later. I don't know who coined the term "trailing spouse," as if one were a piece of loose yarn, waiting to be snipped from a carpet. Around two hundred million people wind about the world for work—highly educated expatriates seeking advancement or shelter from economic storms. One half of a couple chases a job or a promotion and the other half—usually a woman—"trails."

Negotiations between partners are delicate. Careers get juggled, re-balanced, dismantled, broken. There are other issues to consider: children's educations and friendships, aging parents in need of care, property to look after. It's complicated. The winners and losers on Fortuna's Wheel cannot be predicted.

I FIRST FLEW into Chicago during February of 2001. An arctic blast was blowing off Lake Michigan. My heart felt sluggish, pumping icy blood so slowly that I feared my feet and hands would never thaw. The city was bleak, monochrome—not a blade of grass or a leaf to be seen, no break in the clouds, no relief from the slicing wind in my face as I bowed my head and struggled up Wabash Avenue. My husband was interviewing for a position leading a cinema school, a rare job suited to his industry and academic inclinations. Handing over our sons, ages one and seven, to a nanny for their first overnight without us, we left a Southern Hemisphere summer, balmy Auckland, my job and an office view of the Waitemata "sparkling waters." I thought there was no way—*no way*—that I would move if he got an offer.

A remote chance, really.

We didn't write a pro and cons list, negotiate, or think of scenarios in the future. It happened in a shimmer, between me working as a public relations executive, organizing a dump truck-themed second birthday party for my younger boy, and taking my older boy to swimming lessons and rugby practice. Sometimes life seems to happen around you, and like looking into a wobbly mirror, you can't be sure of what you see.

GETTING SUCKED INTO my husband's orbit was a possibility that worried me. He made television shows and films, music videos and plays, played the guitar and read five books a week. I advised clients in a media and communications agency and wrote magazine features on the side. He drove our youngest child to daycare. I led the older son's "walking bus" to elementary school. At seven o'clock, we'd careen back into our bungalow to share the routine of dinner-bath-bed.

Our blooming existed partly because I was not financially dependent on my husband. New Zealand is, or was then, a social democracy with taxpayer-funded support for mothers and babies, subsidized early childhood education, and generous vacation and sick leave, which enabled me to work and have children with relative ease. Work gave me an intellectual high—a friction of deadlines, ideas, and power. It also provided a six-figure salary.

My mother was a single parent. The loss of her husband and the death of her parents when she was a child made my mother poor. Being without, and the accompanying lack of freedom and opportunity, made me nervous. Like Virginia Woolf, I thought about "the safety and prosperity of the one sex and of the poverty and the insecurity of the other."

On the counsel of a financial advisor, I had opened multiple bank accounts, saved for a house, set up investments, bought a house, and paid the mortgage as fast as possible. I'd gone to university and built my career to avoid dependence. In agreeing to move to a new country, I assumed my career would continue. Changing our carefully balanced arrangement made me uncertain, but I thought we'd adapt. Times had changed since Woolf wrote of the patriarchy and the dominance of the professor: "His was the money and the power and the influence." Hadn't they?

We took a risk when we got together, trusting our instincts that it was right even though we'd just left other relationships, working against our friends' six-month-wait rule before leaping afresh. In our first year, we moved in together, had a son, married, and bought a house—in that order. The first lawnmower and barbecue arrived when my husband turned forty. Life was settling down for us: we'd just "done" our bathroom and kitchen. Our firstborn was settled in school. Our second son had progressed from the Babies' Cottage to the Big House at daycare. I'd been promoted to director at work. The circus of career, family, and friends was holding together.

A bit more time to revel in the feeling of life-doesn't-get-better-than-this would have been great—so I told my boss, just days before my husband was offered his new job. Work and family had begun to feel less like a reckless teeter-totter and more like a tentatively balanced tightrope act, quivering somewhat, but balanced. Such simple pleasures were not to be taken for granted. Perversely, we were compelled to kick start the momentum.

MY SENSE OF adventure overrode any qualms in the five months since our first trip to Chicago. Bone-eating cold—forgotten. We had both traveled and worked around the world, but not often together and not with our kids in tow. He had worked extensively in America, but New York and L.A. were the only cities I had visited. (My television cop show-informed view of the country was deficient, I knew.) I was not really a stand-by-your-man kind of woman, ready to drop my own job and friends in a flash, but I was proud of my husband's win. The whirl caught me. "Risk! Risk anything!" wrote my countrywoman Katherine Mansfield. "Do the hardest thing on earth for you. Act for yourself. Face the truth." How can we know what is hard until we are in the pain of it? And once there, how do we confront the truth?

A FEW MONTHS later I cleared my desk, left my office, and cried at going away parties. My colleagues gave me a Barbie doll outfit, a recipe for apple pie, a poem, and a parody of *The Addams Family* theme song:

She is a real lady, with hair so sleek and shiny
A dazzler for us every day, that's Toni Nealie
A wonderful wife and colleague, a mother and good
*   friend indeed*
We all do truly love her, that's Toni Nealie

DIVIDING OUR HOUSEHOLD belongings between a dumpster and cardboard packing boxes, we culled our possessions as we ran one room ahead of the professional packers. Husband's vinyl collection? Dumpster. (We did not know that years later my husband would purchase a vintage record player and spend years re-creating his vinyl collection in our Chicago basement.)

Bed our youngest child was born in? Pack.

Memorabilia from travels: Nepali prayer wheel, South African bottle cap sculpture of a camera operator, jacket embroidered with cowry shells and Pacific motifs? Dumpster.

A hundred boxes of novels and art books? A hundred thousand tiny pirates, soldiers, dinosaurs, stacking blocks, farmyard animals, and Legos? Pacifica paintings? A green plastic salad spinner, albums of photos featuring my children's first steps and first hospital trips, the blue glass fruit bowl Nic and Verity gave us for our wedding, my mother's old pewter vase engraved with a couple kissing before a windmill, vintage bone-handled silverware, Italian plates purchased on vacation? Electrical appliances? We didn't stop to realize that they would not work on American voltage. We hauled out the banal and the cherished alike. Pack. Pack. *Pack.*

The plastic corseted torso I wore as Dolly Parton to a fancy dress party? (I don't recall saying "pack," but it crossed the Pacific in a shipping container.)

Mosaic pot with a heart pattern that a friend made for

our wedding? That we chose to store with a friend, for the time being, until our return from this "sabbatical." My husband had secured a three-year contract. We would return. I knew that.

THEN, OUR FAMILY flew over the oceans, crossing the Tropic of Capricorn, the Equator, the Tropic of Cancer, the South Pacific, the North Pacific, continental America. We sped over the International Date Line and through seven time zones. In flight, there is no regard for the logic of hours, but I would soon discover the tyranny of clock-watching when desperately wanting to talk to my mother, waiting until three in the afternoon for her to wake up seventeen hours ahead of me. Twenty-four hours after departure, a white limo whisked us to Oak Park, Illinois—then got lost. It seemed that we had fallen into the mean streets of a television drama. The night was inky: no moon or stars visible, no lamplight penetrating the thick canopy of trees along the Des Plaines River Road from O'Hare Airport.

Poring over a map, my husband directed the driver. I peered nervously into the dark, searching for gunmen hiding behind the oaks. The driver ignored a detour, driving through a mile of roadwork on Lake Street. She woke the kids, crashing into a road barrier and taking out several traffic cones. We arrived in front of our temporary apartment tower, the orange cones still jammed under the limo's bumper. Where in hell were we?

Oak Park, just across Chicago's city limits, had the

fine prairie homes of Frank Lloyd Wright, Victorian Painted Ladies, elm and oak-lined avenues, and the wide, grassy sidewalks that Ernest Hemingway wrote about with disdain. No nukes, no guns, gays welcome, diversity celebrated—or so we read on the Chamber of Commerce website. Two days later, we headed into the city to explore the Field Museum. Outside the Roosevelt El station was a police stakeout. Helicopters. Roadblocks. A real hostage scenario. This was no television cop drama. We had arrived in America.

All too soon, my husband and second-grader vanished into the secrets of their important work and school days, where they formed fresh relationships and learned new routines. The small human and I were left to get to know our new home. I spent hours staring at shelves of Tide and Purex, o.b. tampons, and Edy's ice cream, searching for a familiar name.

This was a type of aloneness I had never encountered. No familiar friends to talk to, no colleagues, no meetings to rush to. My husband, who used to meet me for lunch or coffee during our working days, was consumed by his new position. I felt abandoned, by all but my toddler. A limpet, he clung to my leg even when I went to the toilet. This was new. He used to be an independent little boy. Now I always had an appendage attached. We spent hours together—at home painting, playing with fire trucks and reading *Hop on Pop*, listening to story time at the library, playing at the tot lot, walking the streets searching for a face that could become familiar. He was too young to hold a conversation and he napped every day. Never before had I so many hours without another adult.

On my birthday, I jammed into a Victoria's Secret fitting room trying on lingerie along with my all-male audience, husband and sons, cheering me on. There were no grandmothers, aunties, neighbors, nor babysitters. In this new life, I set up play dates with moms in a playgroup. The "play date" was new to me. In my old life, friends dropped in unannounced for a cup of tea or called to arrange a beach trip the next day. Now, mothers on the school playground pulled out their organizers to schedule meetings, often a week or a month in advance. We gathered in kitchens that had granite countertops and appliances hidden behind wood paneling. These were middle-class homes that were bigger and fancier and tidier than my friends' homes in New Zealand. They had mud rooms and multiple bathrooms and more plastic toys than I had seen outside of toy shops. We drank drip coffee and watched our small children tussle over dinosaurs and spaceships. At school PTO meetings, I recorded minutes about whiteboard fundraisers and new playground equipment. I did the splits in mom-and-toddler gym 'n' swim classes, conquered Play-Doh and hand painting, and learned to make cupcakes.

SPLITTING, SPLINTERING, LOSING my adherence to secure friendships, to identity, to self-purpose. "It is the reality of the self which we transfer into things. It has nothing to do with independent reality," wrote Simone Weil. When you move away from everything you know, your reality falls away around you. The detachment, the severing, makes the illusion of it all painfully clear. I don't understand why anyone would seek to be detached, to aspire to *see* the illusion. Which images faded first? My terraced garden, with its tall plumes of bamboo and birds singing in the flax bushes. Moonlight streaking the magnolia blooms. The camellia tree under which we buried my youngest son's placenta, to root him in the land. Dear friends, whose children would grow up without my gaze. My son and his pal Eric rolling down the grassy hill in Grey Lynn Park. The drive to work past mangroves and sailboats. Colleagues. Work tasks. Lunching with my favorite client Robyn in a courtyard café. She died of breast cancer several years after I moved.

It becomes harder to summon these *realities* in any tangible way. They are streaky memories, sometimes defined, at other times receding, blurred, wavering.

ALL THE SELVES I had constructed unraveled like an unfastened bandage. Attributes that I thought were fundamental to my being had vanished. I was no one's friend, employee, countrywoman. I was not even a citizen. My familiar identities were oceans away. I grieved for what I had mistaken for self. When the bank manager opening our account wrote down "homemaker" as my occupation, I burst into tears. I gnawed the inside of my cheek. Tendrils of my hair fell out, blocking the shower drain and curling across the floor. My self-image as an independent woman faded.

The bureaucratic landscape changed after the 9/11 terrorist attacks. New policies prevented me from getting a driver's license. The offer of a political speechwriting job slid away because I was unable to get work authorization, despite having a visa to work. Was I sentenced to a life of molding Play-Doh warriors and stringing macaroni necklaces? I left the country a few times—Christmas in London with family, a visit to my son's godmother in Amsterdam, a trip home—and it was always a relief to let my guard down with people who knew me. But that joy and ease was shredded upon my return, when I was hustled through passport control and sometimes into the secondary room for interviewing. My ethnicity, race, and nationality were scrutinized in a way I had not previously experienced. It seemed that I had erred, but I didn't know what my crime was. I felt powerless. Resentment glowed inside me, a line of hot lava under smooth black rock. No travel books or relocation advisors could have alerted me to these possibilities.

THE BAY WINDOW of our second-floor apartment looked onto a quiet street with ornate Queen Anne houses and not much traffic. The morning would start with a glimpse of the woman who jogged around our block so slowly we called her the "sloth lady." Then I would walk my schoolboy to his class, with the toddler in his stroller. Then to Whole Foods for meatballs, bananas, potatoes, carrots, peas, and fish sticks. I'd trudge a mile home with grocery bags hanging off the stroller. After that, make the beds. Unload the dishwasher. Cart the boys' dirty t-shirts, jeans, socks down narrow back stairs to basement. Start laundry. Make sandwiches for lunch. Cut off crusts. Finger paint. Nap. Race to school to fetch my older son. Watch kids on swings in playground. Walk home. Supervise homework. Hustle down to the basement. Put laundry in dryer. Cook the meatballs. Serve children. Clean kitchen. Pick up dirty socks. Run bath. Yell at boys for sloshing water onto floor, where it threatened to seep into our landlord's apartment. Watch teeth cleaning. Find youngest son's blankie. Read *The Man Whose Mother Was a Pirate*. Turn on going-to-sleep-music—Cassandra Wilson's *Blue Light at Dawn*. Dim lights. Go to bed. Get up. Repeat.

EACH DAY I longed for the hour when my husband would return, another adult, familiar, who understood me.

EXCEPT HE DIDN'T, really. Our lives ran on different tracks. His world was expansive, full of novelty, films, filmmakers, and frequent travel. I had no stories to tell. My voice was stuck in my throat. I had expected an adventure, but this was an indentured mess of diapers, fish sticks and chicken nuggets, nose-wiping and whining, the latter mainly mine. How had I become caught in this trap?

"SUBURBAN NEUROSIS" WAS a term first used in the 1930s and popularized in the 1950s. It described the anxiety and sadness of women who moved from cities to tract housing developments on the edges of towns and fields. When women moved far from their mothers, extended families and local support networks of neighbors, they lost their babysitters and sense of community. They raised their children alone while their husbands worked. Isolated women with "new town blues" became weepy, lonely, and bored. Housework becomes drudgery when you do it alone, when it is the focus of your day.

When I complained about not coping, my husband, in a moment of exasperation, asked, "What do you expect me to do about it?" He advised me to be patient. Used to meeting daily work deadlines, I was accustomed to more immediate gratification. Part of me could have traded in the kids and spouse for a new pair of boots—the walking kind. Unlike me, he planned his projects years in advance, and read and wrote meticulously with no obvious end in sight. He probably wondered why he'd flown over the ocean with a hothead.

Magda was my first friend. Polish by nationality, she relocated from Amsterdam with her Dutch husband and their two young children a week before me. We met by chance on the street outside our apartment. Her daughter's colorful tricycle caught my eye. Her son needed a diaper change, so I invited her in. Days later, when the planes careened into the Twin Towers, my family gathered at her house. Strangers in a new land, we mourned without our wider families, trying to make sense of a changing world.

Some days, we cooked meatballs together for early dinners with the children before the men came home. We shivered together on the playground as the weather cooled and the leaves turned brown. Because of post-9/11 security issues and my failed quest for a driver's license, Magda gathered the kids and me in her Honda to shop and go to the park. Friendship stopped me from breaking.

At a party, I overheard my husband tell our new friends that he wanted to stay. I threatened to leave. Divorce had not been in my vocabulary, but lo, there it was, hurling across the room in front of crying children, too late to be scooped back. What had been posed as a sabbatical was now of indeterminate duration, perhaps forever, and I felt pathetically unmoored from all I had known and all that I had been.

I simmered. His life, expanding. My life, shrinking. His: the city, the world. Mine: the suburbs, pre-school, elementary school. Him: a calm house after a stimulating day full of people. Me: small, grubby hands, and loneliness pressing in. He told me I was doing a great job, but I didn't value my role, so his praise felt pointless. Unlike my mother, who felt that her mothering role was pivotal, I did not prize my position. Churlish, perhaps. Some women I knew would have traded their jobs to be at home with their kids. Some women said I was lucky. But this was not my choice; I was a woman who had grown up aware of the power of my own agency.

What does this say about how we divide our labor, that even *I* diminished the work of full-time parenting? My husband advanced his career, got paid, and gained recognition, while I learned what it means to be *just* a mother. Every time I visited our doctor, dentist, or ophthalmologist, they asked what *he* was doing. This is how a woman becomes invisible.

I MISSED MY homeland: the nikau palm outside my window, tui birds on the flax blooms chiming their bell notes to each other at dusk, the volcanic Rangitoto hugging the entrance to Waitemata Harbor, the hibiscus tree behind my kitchen, the ozone smell of the Pacific pounding on the east coast, how sunlight reflecting on the shiny karaka leaves made my eyes crinkle in the brightness. In my nostalgic dreams of New Zealand, there were no traffic jams, difficult clients, timesheets to update, monthly invoices to file, or sick kids that came to work so Mom didn't miss a meeting.

Job contracts don't have a fine print section warning of loss, missing, craving, dissolving, drowning. Relocation guides concentrate on making lists, how to deal with movers, how to find schools, where to have lunch and shop, and which appliances won't work in your new country. Those books, which I didn't think to look at until after we'd moved, couldn't help me. Now there are websites, blogs, and social networks dedicated to expatriates and their spouses, addressing cultural barriers and the "expat blues." Today I read an article posted on a site for Internations, a club of almost two million people. It said I could find balance in my transition by paying attention to the five fundamental aspects in life: health (earth), relationships (water), motivation (fire), reflection (air), and intention (ether). Ha! If only I had known. I did not find my balance for a long time.

THERE ARE MILLIONS of trailing spouses, drifting from Poland to Dubai, Britain to Australia, Jordan to France, the Netherlands to Indonesia, New Zealand to the U.S.A., with or without children, with or without common language, with or without relocation expense accounts and repatriation agreements. Books and blogs can't really tell you how to chart your emotional terrain, how to circumnavigate the currents of loss and longing. They don't tell you that you might gain twenty pounds, about the babies born, the friends who get breast cancer, the children who grow up and graduate, the family members who die, the boss who moves away, the divorces, the second marriages, the mourning and celebration, the trivia and change, all while you are away. No, these are waters you have to map yourself. "I was much further out than you thought / And not waving but drowning," wrote the poet Stevie Smith. Hopefully, the shore holds firm.

SOMEWHERE ALONG THE way in my new life, I righted myself. My thinking shifted. My husband was right about patience, although for a while I begrudged him a wisdom not earned in the trenches of suburbia. My little piece of thread was snipped from a social tapestry that had taken many phone calls and cups of tea to create in my former life. My weft is still firmly knotted in there, but slowly over the years, I've woven myself into a new community and stitched my children in safely.

Am I the same person I was? I don't think so. It becomes harder to go back to my homeland because life has moved on there. My sister moved to Britain forty years ago. As her children grew into adults and had their own families, she became more embedded in British culture. As some choices widen, others narrow. As her world expanded through travel and career choices, so the option of return diminished, like some inviolate law of economics explained with graphs and laser points, but rarely understood.

I didn't initially think about our children's education, as second-culture kids raised away from extended family and the culture they were born into. I didn't think of our future, any future. In my mind I was perennially twenty-seven, with no vision of my husband and I getting older. Along the way, the suspended reality of living in another country had worn off. I know now: this is our life.

I have learned to be resilient without a familiar structure. Act for myself? Face the truth? Risk, risk everything? Who I thought I was, wasn't the entire me. Turns out, I am less of a risk taker, less adaptable than assumed. More needy, less independent. Vulnerable to Fortuna's wheel and the vagaries of change.

Our internal worlds are as uncertain and changing as the world around us. I understand that now. We may think we are our jobs, our houses, our countries, our families, our cars, and our purses, even. When that's stripped away, we are left with seams patched to the best of our ability and a few wayward tufts—strands never quite smoothed.

ON THE RIGHTS
AND PRIVILEGES OF
BEING AN ALIEN

HE LEANS IN against me. Stale neck, faintly damp chest, coffee breath. There's no getting away from his musty warmth. I focus on the yellow and black diamond pattern of my thin cotton dress, my coppery skin denting beneath the fabric as he presses cool metal to my flank. I sink into myself, away from the burn in my cheeks, away from this man pushing the border between outside and in. Don't look as he glides his arm down my back. Don't flinch as he presses my armpit, the back of my knee. Does he feel my swampish fever, the fear percolating to my surface? I've been scanned many times at airports, but never with such strange intimacy. Nearby, shoeless travelers watch their belongings bump along the conveyor belt at O'Hare. The TSA officer's wand slides along the inside of my thigh. He hasn't spoken to me at all.

I flick my brown eyes up, meeting the worried blue eyes of my son across the man's shoulder. The boy's blond hair curls up beyond his now pale temple, his ears flushing at the lobes. The officer pulls away and I feel the air between us. "Who is this woman to you," he demands from my son.

"She's my mother," my son responds. The man glances from my passport to my son's, to him, to me, to him.

We don't look alike. *Do not speak, do not speak, do not speak*, my dark eyes tell my fair boy. The man waves us on.

The woman who stops me by the boarding gate is rougher, bigger, and more aggressive as her hands maneuver across my dress, which is flimsy and covers me snugly. There is no room to conceal anything. Why am I being searched again? I stand off to one side as people enter the air bridge to the plane. My two sons wait close by, one small and dark like me, the other sturdy and fair. We are on our way to join their father, my husband, in Europe where he is teaching a film class for the summer of 2009. All four of us are American permanent residents and citizens of New Zealand—home of cinematic hobbits, champion sailors, a teen pop star and a Man Booker prize-winner. Except I feel as if I am an enemy. My legs are parted, my arms askew, my long brown hair now sticking to my neck, my clavicle, my damp cheeks—my borderlands exposed. Most of the travelers embarking look the other way, or narrow their eyes to take in the general tableau without making eye contact, avoiding the specific, the individual, me. I feel shame, but I'm not sure why. This is security. It's nothing personal, really.

Eight hours of air space, of no man's land, of gazing out into interminable silver, pale horizons that belong to no one, of time limning imaginary divides, cloud drift, the rush of freezing air beyond the windows, and a glimmering sense of freedom. An unwarranted sense of freedom.

A German immigration officer calls me out of line. My

boys are buoyed along ahead by the stream of disembarking passengers ahead of me. She motions me into a cubi-
cle. "But wait, my boys . . . Boys! Boys! Wait! Wait!" They
turn, alarmed, brows lifted, mouths ajar, the little one
clutching for his brother. "My boys, my boys, please . . . "
But she has her wand at the ready, intruding, invading—
the third time this trip. There is no point in resistance. My
tawny skin could be, what, Palestinian, Afghani, Pakistani,
Iraqi? *Enemy*-colored, regardless.

I used to love travel, the idea of being a global citizen.
I grew up in the relative wealth of New Zealand believing
it was my right, a necessity to face outward and embrace
the world. Now that I live and work in the United States,
I find myself questioning the ease of crossing borders,
of the legitimacy of the traveler and the relevance of the
boundaries, the power of bureaucracies, the dangers of
borderland scrutiny, and the insecurities bred by security
and surveillance. Wherever I travel, it seems that something about me invites scrutiny, official inspection. Something about us, the few that are flagged, shuffled into cubi-
cles for an extra pat down, a secondary interview, for the
snap of a rubber glove, to have our luggage and our bodies
rifled through.

I AM AN Alien. I am A54**32. For a time I was a Non-Res-
ident Alien, then I was an Alien on Advanced Parole. I am
now a Resident Alien. The language is peculiar, drum-
ming up recollections of 1950s comics, creatures from

the swamp, pods of extra-terrestrials, unidentified flying objects, reds under the bed, and sci-fi evildoers. Some countries do not use this lexicon at all, instead using neutral terms such as applicant, overseas citizen, visitor, passenger returning and resident. The alien terminology leaves me high and dry, on a continent that feels hostile and prickly.

I am permitted to live in the United States. I am permitted to work and pay income taxes, to pay private insurance for health care, to own a house and pay high property taxes that fund local schools. I am not allowed to vote, a fact unusual to me because New Zealand, along with Great Britain, the Netherlands, Chile, and many countries in between, allows universal suffrage for all residents. I have been obliged to offer up pieces of myself—my eyeballs, my thumbprints, my history, my blood, some of my freedoms, here in the land of the free.

My iris is captured in a biometrics file with the U.S. Immigration Service, photographed by a high-quality digital camera in a Homeland Security outpost in a room with grey vinyl flooring and grey plastic chairs, in a strip mall in Norridge, Illinois. My eyes were filtered and mapped into phasors or vectors. My eyes became a series of successful algorithms. My deep brown eyes, the eyes that have held the gaze of my beloved, that are the color and shape of my mother's, that my newborn sons searched for and struggled to focus on, are now U.S territory.

The iris scan was first used by law enforcement agencies to identify prisoners, but the fingerprint was the earliest forensic biometric record. Loops and spirals were caught in clay in ancient Babylon and China, to keep track of business deals. Prints have been identifying criminals, real and suspected, since the late nineteenth century. In 1924, during the first Red Scare in the U.S., the identification division of the FBI was set up. By the time a second such scare was underway in the forties, the FBI had one hundred million cards blacked with whorls and spirals, lined up in tall filing cabinets. By 1970, two hundred million people had their two prints inked, rolled, and stamped. Now Homeland Security stores more than one hundred and twenty million people's prints, and the FBI has sixty million computerized records, both criminal and civil. All are available to Interpol's network.

My own prints, with my furrows, ridges and valleys, were harvested five or six times. How many times do American authorities need fingerprints? Do they change over time? Do the bad guys change their prints? Sometimes. The 1930s bank robber John Dillinger burned his off with acid and today's criminals alter theirs surgically. My fingers pluck mint from my garden, knead fresh bread, stroke my sons' hair, lace themselves between my husband's—I have not altered them.

IT SEEMS INCONGRUOUS to mention the assault on the Twin Towers and the Pentagon as background to this, to group my own potential criminality with those other swarthy invaders, the ones who pierced airspace, buildings, and human lives. To say it was bad timing to move to the United States weeks before, though, seems callous. I don't want to trivialize the horror of that day. Nonetheless, it locked me into eight years of cyclic fingerprinting, assignations in federal buildings shielded by concrete barriers and teeming with holstered security guards, appointments in strip malls, searches in airports, and a lag of five years between my husband and children getting permanent residency and me finally being able to use the same line in the airport as my family. This altered my perception of myself to a woman vulnerable to the hands of airport authorities, to a person of color profiled as a possible enemy, to a foreigner with ambiguous status. The "security" of the greater good has become my shaky insecurity.

Being viewed as a potential threat fractures you, diminishes you. You begin to suspect your own legitimacy, your place in the long, snaking lines of mainly brown people waiting for their numbers to come up. Are you trying to sneak into a society that doesn't want you? Are you in the shadows of illegality? Could they deport you? Could they separate you from your children? Could they make you disappear?

If you've ever been in a secondary interrogation room in an American port of entry, you will recognize this fear. The large room is walled off from the main passport control hall that travelers snake through after disembarking.

Uniformed border officers perch up behind a high counter looking down at rows of weary arrivals slouched in plastic chairs. There are a few citizens, but most are tourists or expatriates or immigrants. There is no privacy. Yelling, crying, pleading, and sometimes urinating take place in full view and earshot of those waiting for their passport to come to the top of the pile. It's a morality play in the public square, except we are an unwilling and undemonstrative audience.

There's the vacationing Italian whose travel agent has not informed him that even though Italy is a friendly nation with a visa waiver, he should have a passport with an electronic chip or a current visa. When the officers finally dismiss him, he protests their treatment and tries to argue. "Do you want to leave, or shall we put you on the next plane back to Italy?" He leaves.

There's the English student planning a Transamerica road trip for six weeks, but he's visibly of Asian heritage, so they hector him about why he's on vacation for so long, and how did he get that time off work? He explains that he has left his job, because he's a student, and besides, in the U.K. most workers get six weeks paid leave, but they don't believe him. They harangue him for forty-five minutes before letting him go.

There's the Fijian-born Indian New Zealander with a U.S. green card who says she was in New Zealand for six months because her brother was killed in a motorbike crash and she stayed longer to help her aging mother. She quietly weeps, laying out her grief before a room of witnesses uncomfortable with this uninvited intimacy.

A Chinese woman speaks via a translator. The officer asks if she has a child. She says no. After fifteen minutes of questioning, the officer calls a colleague over.

"Why are you lying?" they ask.

"I'm not lying," she repeats.

"The computer tells us you have an eight-year-old daughter. Why deny it?" They take turns berating her, yelling at her.

The translator is flustered, frantic, near tears. "But we misunderstood you," the translator pleads. "We thought you meant did she have a child *with* her, is she *traveling* with her child, but her daughter is with her grandparents in China. It was confused in *translation*."

There is a *secondary*, secondary interview room, where body searches take place. I have not yet had that experience.

I WAS ON advanced parole for years. I was not held against my will, but sometimes I felt unduly confined. How did I get to this limbo? The process started not long after we moved in 2001 for my husband's job, as a department chair in a large college. We were pressed into the permanent residency process for employment reasons, so my husband could travel freely to international conferences and business meetings. He seemed to have moved to a different country than me, his experience was so different, so smooth, benign and friendly. He got a social security number and driver's license immediately, a bank account, and within a couple of years, he, and our children, had permanent residency.

I didn't achieve residency until the last days of December in 2008. I don't know why. Maybe because my last name was different to my husband's, or because I hadn't secured my social security number before 9/11, or maybe because I was brown, or because something in my application had raised a red flag. I'd been convicted and fined $25 for stealing a can of tuna when I was a student. I'd had my wisdom teeth removed under the influence of Valium and left the store with a can in one hand and my wallet in the other. (Under the Clean Slate Act, it no longer appears on my record in my homeland, but I've illuminated my crime forever with the U.S Immigration Service.)

The tenor of the questions in that application took me by surprise. Maybe I was naïve, having moved from a country with no perceived external threats, little government corruption, four million people and seventy thousand sheep. The questions had a film noir quality, a hangover from a more sinister age. I thought of the McCarthy era, the Hollywood blacklists and the House Committee on Un-American Activities. I did un-American things most days: I pronounced schedule with a soft "sh." I scoffed at my son reciting the Pledge of Allegiance at school. I struggled to understand the partnership between peanut butter and jelly. But there was no subversion in our suburban life.

The forms asked: *Have you ever been a member of a communist organization?*

No. (Although when I was at university I went out with a dude in the student chapter of the New Zealand Workers Communist League. Is that paranoia?)

Have you ever been a member of a terrorist organization?

No. (Protesting against the Springbok rugby tour against the All Blacks? Concrete down a toilet at a feminist rally?)

Have you ever committed a crime of moral turpitude?

Moral turpitude has been in U.S. immigration law since 1891, but isn't defined by statute (though State Department regulations try to clarify it), and doesn't feature in other countries, so I pondered this carefully.

Have you been guilty of conduct that is considered contrary to community standards of justice, honesty or good morals?

How do you determine the depths of your *turpitude?* Stabbing Peter Fellows in the leg with a freshly sharpened pencil because he wouldn't stop swinging on the back of my chair in fourth grade? Sticky-ing the living room floor with booze when my mother was out of town, dumping the bottles in the church trash bin across the road, lying that I was at my friend's house? Telling my sister's boyfriend that my sister cheated on him when he was sick with mono? Sleeping with a boyfriend's brother? Having three boyfriends at the same time, dismissing one out the window while another was knocking at the door? Failing to act when, as a camp counselor, a nine-year-old girl confided that she had been raped by her uncle?

I was unjust, dishonest, and had dodgy morals. But I grew up. Was there a statute of limitation?

Overall, I thought I was a good person. I was kind to friends and made my kids clean their teeth after eating sweets. I believed in the common good and paid my taxes in full. I had adopted two rescue cats. I checked *No*. I had not committed crimes of moral turpitude.

IN THE WEEKS and years after 9/11 everything was jammed up and panicked. My husband had secured basic documents like a driver's license and social security number as soon as we had arrived, while I focused on settling in the children, who were two and seven. I, who had been a journalist, editor, and public relations advisor all my adult life, was for the first time a "homemaker." I had a visa to work, but no work authorization, and could not get one in any reasonable time, so I declined several job offers. I waded into uncertainty, bureaucracy, hyper-vigilance. I couldn't drive my children because I couldn't get a driver's license because that would require a social security number. I couldn't get a social security number because that would require a letter from the Department of Transportation, which would provide one only if I had a social security number. I rocketed backward and forward for days between two departments. I met others in a similar position—expatriate spouses of foreign lawyers, business advisors and consultants hired by international corporations and big agencies—trapped stateside with a driving prohibition that made us feel akin to women in Saudi Arabia.

MY LOVE AFFAIR is with my husband, not my adopted country, or the gatekeepers. I am here like so many international families of the so-called *knowledge economy*. I came as a package of four. As much as I know terrorism is a threat, I also know my kids are more likely to die by beer, prescription drugs, a gunshot, drowning, a speeding Ford, a tainted cantaloupe or a bad hot dog at a Cubs game. I worry about my sons as they become old enough to travel without parents. Will the blond, blue-eyed son be waved on, while his dark-eyed, tawny brother is held back?

My discomfort is incomparable to those fleeing persecution or poverty. We sat side by side on grey chairs in featureless waiting rooms that smelled inexplicably of classroom chalk, school raincoats, and urine. We were all again children, powerless before authority. It made little difference that my homeland was not an engorged or war-torn country, not one that racist politicians froth about, or one with ambiguous and contested boundaries. Aotearoa, New Zealand, is ostensibly a friend of America, part of its surveillance network and a historic ally. I thought that gave me immunity. I used to be secure in my privileged, middle-class spot in a safe, harmless, faraway country. I'm ashamed to say that at first I wanted to set myself apart from the others, to shriek: "You started it! You flirted with my husband first! You courted us, you encouraged us from the other side of the world, and this is how you treat me?" Like those I waited alongside, my skin color signaled more about my immigration status than my passport. I am a brown-skinned daughter of Aotearoa and the South Pacific, a grandchild of India and Great Britain, a mother, a wife, a writer, a friend, and more. Resident, not alien.

THE DARK-SKINNED
DISPENSER OF REMEDIES

I'M PEELING POTATOES for dinner in Chicago, the phone clamped between my ear and shoulder, talking to my mother as she has her morning tea. A chilly wind is blowing up from the Southern Ocean, she says, so she hasn't wandered up the road to get her groceries. Her old bones get creaky if she doesn't walk every few days. I imagine her, seventeen hours ahead of me, sitting in her rose-patterned Sanderson linen chair, drinking Earl Grey from a pale blue and white china cup. Age is pressing in on her. Glaucoma narrows her life now, so she walks to the store or down the track to the beach, but usually keeps close to her small brick house. I want to ask about my grandfather again, but I can't bear stirring her up so that she'll fret later, alone. She has always avoided talking about her father.

"Don't let anyone know that's your grandfather in there," she'd murmur when I was a child walking with her past his mausoleum. She hated him. He was cruel. "He sent my mother home to her family to die. He threw her out because she didn't have sons." This is what I heard growing up, not understanding why a man wouldn't want daughters.

When she was three, my mom lost her mother. By

twelve, she was an orphan. "I miss Mother," is a frequent refrain in our long-distance conversations.

I press on.

MOST FAMILIES HAVE secrets, the clichéd skeletons in the closet. As technology hastened access to old records, my family's rattling bones began somersaulting out from the media. Fifty years after his death, my grandfather featured in a television show, then in books, in an online encyclopedia—and now in blogs and websites. Each source replicates much unattributed information, impossible to verify because no one, other than my mother, is alive to comment. All that my mother kept hidden about her father is now in plain sight.

From my safe distance in America, I could afford to poke away, to search for nuances and context and points of view. On moving here, I was profiled at the border and shunted into a years-long immigration process very different from my husband's seamless transition. In the aftermath of 9/11, amid a wash of anti-Muslim and anti-immigrant sentiments, I confronted my heritage. My cultural roots were in Aotearoa, New Zealand, but my skin, hair, and eyes favored my Indian grandfather. Unmoored from siblings, friends, and full-time work, I had time to investigate my family's past. I was out of my mother's range, so I wouldn't embarrass her. She was getting older. I was running out of years to ask questions. The time had come to sniff out what had been suppressed.

If my grandfather's ghost refused to stay silent, perhaps it was time to claim him.

MY GRANDFATHER IS persistent. He died in 1941, long before my birth, yet he knocks for attention still. I have carried him around in photographs and letters and newspaper clippings for years. He lives in a drawer next to my desk, in a manila envelope filed between my sons' school report cards and travel soccer roster. Every so often I take him out and put him away again. Each year there is more of him.

In a fragile sepia photograph, Wally Salaman looks stern in a topcoat and fob watch, peering out over pince-nez spectacles. "I was only a boy of fourteen when I left India," he wrote in a letter to a relative. Sailing away from family, he arrived in New Zealand in 1903. An importer of precious stones, silks and carpets, he dabbled in real estate and made aniline fabric dyes for soldiers' khaki in World War One, under contract to the government. Grandpa Salaman gained fame—and notoriety—as an herbalist, on the wrong side of the law. So many views of him exist that I feel like a game show competitor trying to press the buzzer for the best answer. Was he a:

a) bold adventurer,

b) charlatan,

c) successful businessman,

d) devout Muslim,

e) non-practitioner who staged a Muslim funeral as afterlife insurance,

f) family man who left generous trust funds for
  his descendants,

g) cad who abandoned two wives because they
  bore girls,

h) victim of 1920s colonial racism,

i) dangerous criminal, a child killer?

I didn't need to fossick in dusty library records for his trail. Turning on my computer, I came across newly digitized newspaper records from the 1920s and 1930s. The headlines blared:

> *Salaman in Court. Indian Herbalist. Salaman on Trial.*
> *Why Salaman Came to Court. Herbalist faces Grave*
> *Charges. Salaman Case. Tragic story at Manslaughter*
> *Trial. Accused of Murder. Charge Against Indian. Ills of*
> *the Flesh. Recommend Mercy. Will Salaman Be Released?*
> *Fraud! Ruffian! Humbug! Salaman Swindler.*

My grandfather killed a child. No—a child died while under his care in 1930. No—my grandfather *denied* treating him at all. Six-year-old Lyall Christie was ill for four years. Two medical doctors treated him for diabetes. His mother took him to my herbalist grandfather. Two days later little Lyall died. Convicted of manslaughter, my grandfather was sent to prison for a year's hard labor. These are the facts, baldly stated.

I doubt that my grandfather was responsible for the

boy's death. The more I read about the period, the more I find unvarnished racism and a colonial medical establishment protecting itself. Tabloid newspaper *New Zealand Truth* said the case was "a poignant story told by the dead child's mother, Mary Ann Christie: a narrative of childish illness and suffering over a period of years with the tragic knowledge confronting the parents that their young son was, according to one doctor, doomed to die at a young age."

The boy's mother testified that she saw my grandfather as a last resort, trying anything for her ailing child. She paid no fee and received no medicine. In court she said, "I wouldn't like to blame him for the boy's death."

I FUMBLED MY way through newspaper records back to the 1920s. Earlier attempts to convict my grandfather failed. In 1924, a nine-year-old Māori girl named Mane Reiha died. She was in the hospital for a month. When doctors said nothing more could be done for the child, her grandmother took her to the herbalist. My grandfather sold the woman four bottles of a "tonic" containing quinine, almond oil, and herbs.

The magistrate: "He mixed it up with as much skill as a barman mixes a cocktail."

The Health Department doctor: "Oh, that usually requires some skill."

The magistrate called my grandfather a ruffian and a humbug. "Go back to India and practice on your own people," he advised. A Health Department doctor said that when Māori people "hear of the 'marvelous Indian doctor,' they come to him from long distances, especially with cases practically hopeless; the patients die; then the trouble begins."

Cost, not mortality, was the Health Department's concern. "The relatives go to an undertaker, but have no death certificate, Salaman not being in a position to give one. That is how our Department comes to hear of the cases. The result is a coronial inquiry, a coffin has to be procured, the body sent back home—all this *expense* has to be borne by the Health Department, when the patient should have been left to die in peace in his own district."

The doctor who did the post-mortem on Mane Rei-ha certified that the child had died of tuberculosis. My grandfather had *not* killed her.

LATER THAT YEAR, Salaman returned to court for a jury trial. Agnes Stewart, a nurse with medical, surgical and midwifery qualifications, claimed damages for negligent treatment. She saw many doctors for goiter before going to the herbalist. My grandfather gave her tonics containing potassium iodine and opium. Her friend, also a nurse, testified that Stewart said she was on her deathbed. She was "in a most shocking state, in a desperate way, so desperate that he did not want to take the case at all."

Salaman's wife, my grandmother, was a witness. She was described in news reports as "his white wife." Race was clearly an issue. Counsel for the defense felt the need to remind the jury that Salaman was "a colored man, but that fact must exercise not prejudice, as British justice was for all." The defense maintained there was no evidence of harm, and one of the most famous medical authorities also recommended opium. The lawyer for the plaintiff argued that Salaman had traded on his "blackness" by putting in his window a sign "Indian Herb Atah." He said it was inconceivable that a white man would have attracted such a "horde of dupes and hypnotized patients."

Convicted and ordered to pay costs for pretending to be a doctor, my grandfather was sentenced to a month in prison for attempting to receive money by false pretenses. Agnes Stewart died shortly after.

In 1927, he faced six charges of false pretenses when two policemen posed as customers. Salaman examined them with a stethoscope to their throats and magnifying glass to their eyes, they testified. He diagnosed ulcers and poor circulation. The policemen left with assorted bottles of medicine and boxes of pills. When analyzed they were found to contain phenacitin, an analgesic used widely at the time, and small amounts of herbs.

The newspaper described my grandfather as "the dusky one," and "the dark-skinned dispenser of remedies." He was found guilty and fined twenty pounds on the first two counts and convicted for the others. His stock in trade and twelve of his properties were confiscated. He petitioned the House of Representatives, seeking the appointment of a commission to investigate the prosecutions.

On a day when *Truth*'s lead was "Gay Girls Take Wrong Turn/Bacchus Enthroned in Venus Street/Fair Flappers And Business Men in Wild Midnight Orgy," the paper ran a story about Salaman. It compared him to several famous healers. James Moore Hickson was an Australian-born Anglican who traveled the world with his healing ministry. Émile Coué was a French pharmacist who pioneered hypnosis and autosuggestion and famously said, "Every day in every way, I'm getting better and better." Gipsy Smith was a popular evangelist who led a march of thousands to protest Chicago's vice district. Unlike those three, my grandfather's error lay in dealing "with material matter instead of spiritual." He made the mistake of thinking that "it was possible to cure the sick and afflicted by means of drugs and herbs as if they had that essential to all who would be cured—faith." If he had merely stuck to the role of psychic healer, laying on of hands or autosuggestion, he could have avoided trouble.

"He would never have done that," says my mother. "He *believed* in his healing abilities and his medicine."

By contemporary Western standards, my grandfather's herbal methods appear dubious. Te Ara, the national encyclopedia of New Zealand, lists him as a "Merchant, dyer, herbalist, charlatan."

Charlatan. I was indignant. What kind of person can boast that their forebear was a charlatan, a fraud, a fake?

This did not fit with my childhood fairytale about a handsome prince wooing his fair bride. My hands got clammy, my cheeks flushed. If I could un-see the headlines! I snapped shut the computer. A year slid by, then I couldn't find my files, either the paper copies or those stored on my computer. It was as if my mind had redacted the stories. Searching afresh, I found new items, blog posts and web entries, repeated, repeated. None questioned the first telling. Not a journalist challenged the facts, investigated the context, the practices, the times. Once a story has been released, there's no getting it back.

THE VACCINES AND antibacterials we take for granted were not around in the 1920s. Penicillin was discovered in 1928, the year my mother was born. Most cultures have healing traditions based in plant cures. Ayurvedic medicine has been practiced in India for five thousand years. European monks and nuns used herbs, including opium and cannabis. Chinese immigrants brought medicines, acupuncture, massage and meditative exercise. In New Zealand, rongoā Māori—traditional indigenous healing—used remedies from roots and leaves until the Tohunga Suppression Act of 1907 outlawed native healers. In the 1920s, the famous All Black rugby player, George Nepia, was apparently advised to have an operation for a leg injury, but instead he turned to Māori herbal medicine, which worked. The British doctor admitted later that he had not believed the leg could be healed.

Herbal remedies, homeopathy and other alternatives to traditional medicine are widely available today. I'm skeptical of their efficacy, but, unless a practice is found to be directly harmful, a practitioner is unlikely to be imprisoned. It is difficult to judge my grandfather with a modern yardstick. He was tremendously popular with his patients, who gave him gold and bronze medals inscribed with details of his successful treatments.

"When I was six, if I looked out the window on Tuesdays and Wednesdays, I would see cars lining either side of Gill Street," my mother recalls. "Cars with running boards and canvas hoods. People came from all over the country to see him. He didn't take appointments, it was first come, first serve, so they just had to wait. If they missed out, they had to come back another time."

RACISM RIPPLED THROUGH the prosecution of my grandfather. He was a British citizen of colonial India when he arrived in New Zealand, also a British colony at the time. The 1901 census listed only twenty-four "Asiatics." By 1916, the numbers had risen to 181 and grew steadily higher. A cartoon from 1917 shows a British politician opening the door for a "Hindoo," as all Indians, regardless of religion, were called. The caricatured head is turbaned, black-faced, and huge.

By the 1920s, immigration was restricted. The racist White New Zealand League excluded Indians from leadership roles and lobbied to keep immigration white. This is the environment in which my grandfather married my white New Zealand grandmother, conducted his businesses, and went to trial.

THE RACISM WAS not veiled: "The coon in question has been judged a false alarm and a fraud."

The coon. Saying it makes me queasy. I pace around the house with the word souring my mouth. I scrub the white tiles in the shower and load the dishwasher, check my email messages. My fingers are sore from squeezing them.

This ugly word. I was familiar with its use during and after slavery, in the so-called coon songs of Tin Pan Alley, the Rip Coon minstrels, the song "All Coons Look Alike To Me," by Ernest Hogan, and the coon movies that stereotyped African-Americans as lazy, stupid, shiftless, and untrustworthy. Hearing it applied to my Indian grandfather, I realized how racism had seared my mother, how it distorted her views about heritage.

The word's origins are blurry; sources say it comes from raccoon, or maybe from the Portuguese word barracão, which at one time described a shed for housing slaves. It wasn't heard in New Zealand when I grew up, but my high school boyfriend heard it when he first flew to Australia, 2,500 miles away. He hitchhiked across the continent from Sydney to Perth in a truck, a trip that took four days. One night on the arid Nullarbor Plain, the driver hit something. "It's probably just a coon," he laughed, meaning an indigenous person. My boyfriend was so shaken that he called me from a pay phone as soon as he arrived in Perth. Another friend visiting Mparntwe, Alice Springs, in the Northern Territory was horrified to see signs hanging in bars that read, "No Coons Served Here." It was the 1980s and the Arrernte nation had lived in the area for an estimated 40,000 years.

Other offensive words were used in New Zealand, such as "boonga" (a Māori), "coconut" (a Pacific Islander), "curry-muncher" (an Indian), but not "coon." That word carried the weight of slavery and segregation with it, and the idea of a person being a wild animal. To see it in print, in the public record, about my grandfather makes me short of breath.

Racist reports about my grandfather dated back to the end of his first marriage. One described him as a dark-hued Syrian and another as a Hindu, even though he was an Indian Muslim. A *Truth* reporter wrote in 1918: "A young woman who had seen fit to disregard Kipling's advice about the impossibility of East and West mingling . . . proved that her case was no exception." Salaman petitioned for custody of his first child, because his ex-wife was living with a Chinese man. Depending on which side's case was presented, the couple was on "improper terms," or the man was merely a housekeeper. It was a scandal.

Her lawyer said, "This is a new class of case. This country has never before been troubled by the half-caste question." The judge responded, "We have had our half-castes."

"Yes," said the lawyer, "but they were, so to speak, our own people. We have not had Asiatic half-castes." The judge replied that if there were good Chinamen, there were probably good Indians, and the child might be as well be with the father as with the mother. Salaman gained custody. He later married my grandmother Gladys and fathered two more children, my mother and her younger sister.

I FOUND MY grandfather in books—*Lawbreakers & Mischief Makers: 50 Notorious New Zealanders* in a chapter titled "Swindlers, Tricksters & Charlatans" and *King of Stings: The Greatest Swindles from Down Under*. He turned up in magazines and blogs such as *The NZ Listener*, *India-link*, *Waymark*, in library websites and Toastmaster meetings. There is even a story in a current affairs magazine where I once worked. A former colleague wrote it, without knowing I was the granddaughter of his subject.

The hidden part of my family's history was under my nose in the fusty libraries of newspapers where I worked my first journalism jobs. If I had peered into their creaking filing cabinets I may have found the stories glued onto white sheets, or in crumbling newspapers hanging from wooden clasps. It didn't occur to me then to search out the story. I was too busy creating my present to worry about the past.

AFTER SALAMAN WAS convicted, people turned out to support him at public meetings in several towns. One gathering had five hundred attendees. Appreciative patients wrote letters telling of his care. Many felt that the local medical profession was responsible for the severity of his sentence. They petitioned the government for his release, to no avail. He went to prison for a year.

His wife Gladys—my grandmother—died of tuberculosis, and his baby daughter—my mother's little sister—died of diphtheria.

READING BACK THROUGH the old newspaper reports, I am struck by the determination of the authorities to nail him, without evidence that he was acting outside the laws of the time. He never claimed to be a pharmacist or a doctor. Did he believe in his remedies or was he offering placebos? Was he a quack or was he a fraud?

The Latin etymology for *placebo* is "I will please." My grandfather did please people. Placebos have been documented to benefit patients, but their use presents the ethical quandary of knowingly deceiving people when they are vulnerable. What about his use of opium in his "tonics"—did that make him a charlatan? Opium has been used since the Stone Age, in Greek, Persian, Arab, and Western medicine. In the nineteenth and early twentieth centuries, anyone could buy it in tinctures and tonics, in patent medicines, in soothing syrups for babies, which were available at fairs, general stores, and pharmacies. Doctors were able to prescribe much larger doses, until regulations were introduced to deter them.

"Opium is in virtually universal use throughout India as the commonest and most treasured of the household remedies accessible to the people," said Sir William Meyer in a 1912 address to the United Nations. "It is taken to avert or lessen fatigue, as a specific in bowel complaints, as a prophylactic against malaria (for which its relatively high anarcotine content makes it specially valuable), to lessen the quantity of sugar in diabetes and generally to allay pain in sufferers of all ages."

New Zealand medical doctors prescribed opium so liberally that by the 1940s the nation had one of the world's highest rates of use. New Zealand's Quackery Prevention Act tried to prevent people making false claims about their medicines, but many drugs were not regulated until decades later. Ingredients did not have to be listed until 1946, after my grandfather's death.

FOR YEARS I didn't discuss with my mother what I found on the Internet. She felt tied to her father's transgressions. Ignoring him and denying her connection to him was the only way she could carry on. Mortify, from Middle English, to deaden, to subdue by self-denial. My mother tried to protect my siblings and me. She immersed herself, and her children, in the genealogy of her mother's people, the Waltons of County Cork and the Richards of Cornwall. She read me adventure stories about English school children, the *Famous Five* and *Secret Seven*. I grew up knowing Victorian poetry and Māori legends, but nothing of my Indian heritage or our extended family. My mother built a scaffold of rules for my family. Never put the butter on the table without a butter dish and butter knife. Never put the milk on the table without a jug. Never use tea bags. They're vulgar. Ideas of propriety—designed to protect us, to deliver us into respectability. Now I understand.

I resist absorbing her shame and muddle through my conflicting impulses. When I was small, my mother used to walk my siblings and me up to the Shirley Methodist Church every Sunday. At Sunday school I sang "Jesus Wants Me For A Sunbeam" and "Jesus Loves Me, This I Know." The Bible has plenty to say on punishment, including Ezekiel 18: 20, "The son shall not suffer for the iniquity of the father, nor the father suffer for the iniquity of the son. The righteousness of the righteous shall be upon himself, and the wickedness of the wicked shall be upon himself." My mother and I *should* inherit no blame.

I ferret about the Bible and get confused. Exodus 20:5, Job 21:19, and Numbers 14: 18 allow the price of a crime to be felt for several generations, the Law of Moses says a goat can be sacrificed as a kind of atonement proxy, and Christians believe that Jesus made the ultimate sacrifice to wipe our grubby slates clean. I have no goats, and I haven't taken Jesus as my savior, so I'm not sure where I stand there.

My mother never saw her father pray and wasn't sure if he was a believer. The Qur'an says: "Every soul earns only to its own account; no soul laden bears the load of another." There is a judgment day scale that weighs good deeds against bad. Maybe my grandfather's good deeds would help balance his ledger, dying fabric for soldiers' uniforms in World War One, donating land for a public reserve.

ON THE PHONE between America and New Zealand, I made my mother go back to her childhood, to peel off the scab. For eighty-seven years she carried her pain inside her, and covered it up so her children could prosper, untainted by our grandfather's record.

"When I was at school, the teachers would stop talking when I walked by, so I knew they were talking about me," she said. "Children called me a nigger. I was so ashamed. If I ignored it all, maybe I could forget."

In my mother's memories, she is often held aloft, her feet not touching the ground. In one, a stranger holds her above her mother's coffin and tells her to say goodbye one last time. In another, she pictures her father in a small room. She is lifted up and greets him through a window. Now she realizes he was in prison. She recalls leaving New Zealand for India, seeing her father's car hoisted up onto the ship by crane. As the ship crossed the equator, a sailor lifted her and she kicked her feet against him, until one tiny slipper flew off and she watched it tossing in the wake.

So much loss. My mother always said that her father was a bad man. "I remember him hitting me in the bathroom, his razor strop on the back of my legs," she told me. She thought that was because he was Muslim. I reminded her that "Spare the rod and spoil the child," was a common Christian sentiment and that she had spanked me with a wooden hairbrush when I was a child. I don't spank my children because it's mean, but a lot of people do still, regardless of their religion. I don't want to defend her father, nor do I want to support a prejudice.

She grew up believing that her father divorced his first wife because she didn't provide him a son and that he sent my grandmother Gladys away because she too bore only girls. He had sent her back to her family to die, so the story went. Who told my mother that? I wasn't so sure when I read the newspaper clippings. If he only valued boys, it didn't make sense that he fought a bitter, public battle for custody of his first daughter. When my grandmother was dying, he was already in prison. He was in no position to care for her. Would it not be prudent for her to go home to her parents? Where was the compassion of the court, when a man's wife was dying and his little girls were left parentless? My mother, who was loved by her mother's family, absorbed a narrative that no doubt reflected their biases and those of their times.

CHILDREN HAVE NO responsibility for crimes of a previous generation, I believe, but societies *are* culpable. My emotional string is taut. I recoil from my examination, the taint of criminality and the coon-ness of it. I am mortified at this affront to my family heritage. I had filled in the silences in my family story by inventing a fairytale. Now, no amount of imagination brings back the prince that I imagined my grandfather to be, the romance, the magic carpet. It's time to retire the motley remnants of my fantasy, a chewed-up rug that flies nowhere.

Why even concern myself now with any of this? We may all have unreliable biographies, but I think my grandfather deserves to be fleshed out, to be more than a caricature, a crime entry. Like me, he was an alien in a foreign country at a time when paranoia about outsiders was high. I want to claim my Indian heritage, for my children and me. I care about my mother, a fierce keeper of secrets, sheltering me from phantoms and bogeys until I was old enough to shout at them. It took my own isolation to empathize with hers. I care about her—a lonely little girl who lost her family to prison and disease and endured humiliation by racism. She finally gets to share her burden. The child grows up to protect the mother.

MEDITATIONS ON BROWNNESS

I CANNOT BEAR the color brown. I dislike the murkiness of a spent teabag staining the sink, of walls painted North Creek or Middlebury. The hue of sparrows fluffing their feathers in a pool of sandy dirt outside my kitchen window is disagreeable. Clothes in earthy tones depress me. They blur the place where the garment stops and my dark skin begins. I don't want to be lost in brown, don't want to wear what I am.

When faced with checking a box to declare my color—on an airline ticket form, say, or my son's school "race validation"—I have two options: black or white. The choices do not include tan, chocolate, café au lait, a little-sallow-today, ashy-when-unmoisturized, or brick-red after sun exposure.

I do not *desire* brown. I have never loved it or hoarded it, the way some people crave scarlet or jade, collecting cherry scarves or green ceramic bowls. Maggie Nelson writes: "And so I fell in love with a color—in this case, the color blue—as if falling under a spell." But while I am under a spell of sorts, I am not in love. Yellow offers optimism. Celestial blue, hope. Gray signifies melancholy. But brown offers no such clarity. It's a take-it-or-leave-it color. A color I step around.

I WONDER IF my loathing disguises a denial of self, an objection to my own skin and hair and eyes. So I begin to confront the color, seek it out, watch out for it in trees and stones and bodies around my city. I meditate on it, and me. I ponder its aesthetic and the baggage it carries. Of course, brown objects are different than brown people— and most of the world's people are some shade of brown. We do not fit well with the binary of black and white.

If I peer through the streaming shower into the fogged up mirror, my reflected skin is rich amber. Translucent honey when I turn to catch the light filtering through the opaque bathroom window, stippled darkly where water flecks and splatters. My belly is pooled vanilla, my arms cinnamon, bruising into damson at the wrists, my hair freshly brewed espresso. I admire myself, turning in the flow, appreciating the shine of skin, the gleam and warmth of my brown body. I *like* my hues.

Outside of my own skin, beyond it, I'm uncertain how my brownness is perceived by others. The rules are not spelled out. Wading into the pool of ethnicity and race, I cannot decipher the meaning in the ripples and eddies there. What indicates danger? What distrust? What kinship? In unfamiliar social settings, I navigate the shoals of etiquette cautiously, taking care not to run aground. One must be polite, but language games have indistinct parameters. "There is no such thing as race," I'm told. "Race is a social construct." "Ethnicity is more important." "I don't see color." "What are you?" I am bewildered by brown.

WHEN I WAS a child, I wore the color once: an umber twill skirt crafted by my sister, seven years older than me. I had nothing to wear for a third grade field trip to hunt for tadpoles at a local farm. My mother, a widow, had no spare cash to buy me pants, so my sister cut down her own skirt to fit me. She stayed up into the night, pushing the knee control of our ancient Elna sewing machine. On my way to school, I twirled proudly before my friend Janet, but her blond coiffed mother said all the girls would be wearing *pants*. My heart slunk into a petulant sulk of non-belonging, my differences falling in brown folds around my shins. Janet's mother saved me; she loaned me a pair of Janet's pants. I crammed the skirt into my school bag and stalked tadpoles in dirty ponds, secure in the conformity of borrowed blue stretch pants. When I arrived home, buoyant with belonging, my mother glared. "Never tell your sister," she made me promise. *Never* was her amulet against hurt and exclusion. I felt the weight of that betrayal for years, a denial of sisterhood, of origin, of difference, of family.

When we were young, my siblings and I joked about our different shades. We told my freckly white sister that she was adopted, while she insisted I'd been dropped in the coal bucket when I was a baby. I hear the echo of five-year-olds on the asphalt playground, calling to me "Brownie, hey, Brownie." I was caramel to their pink and white marshmallowness. Our teacher saw our differences, too, and reinforced a color divide in the classroom. The only other brown child there was Edward, who smelled musty and spoke in halting, fractured vowels and blurred consonants. Blackboards lined the classroom, and Edward and I practiced our wavering cursive shoulder to shoulder, conjoined by our skin color. We were the only two children in the class who had to share a blackboard; we finished our practice coated in finely powdered chalk dust, ghosted replicas of our classmates.

I grew up in New Zealand as a post-colonial child in all but my imagination. In my child's mind, I was blond. I was Guinevere, riding down Fitzroy Avenue on the back of Lancelot's white steed, my golden tresses rippling behind me like a victory pennant, my violet eyes flashing with the passion of an Arthurian legend. My internal mirror reflected the pale complexions of the heroines in the books I read and the movies I saw, reflected the fair face of my beloved French teacher, who had eyes the color of oceans and corn silk hair that hung down past her hips; I wanted to be her. I never had a teacher that looked like me. The only dark dolls I ever saw were touristy caricatures, plastic Māori maidens wearing flax skirts.

AT UNIVERSITY AND as I began my career, I saw few people who looked like me. I rarely thought about my brownness, unless someone made me think of it. A boyfriend's mother prohibited him from being with me because of my "background," but I wasn't clear what she meant. A national television news editor said he already had two "darkies" on the staff and didn't need any more. I let implications slide off me, as if I had a sleek carapace that would not, could not, be pierced. I didn't examine color, my color. I was young, tumbling on into my future, protected by confidence and optimism.

I struggled to explain to friends, who insisted, "You're just like us," that somehow I wasn't quite, even though I also was. I listened to the same music, watched the same movies, fumbled through first loves, met similar milestones in work and relationships, but I didn't look the same.

Strangers sometimes treat me differently, depending upon where I am. Sometimes I've been mistaken for kin—a member of the Love family from Taranaki in New Zealand—or for a member of the same tribe—a friend from Salamanca in Spain, an Indian cousin, an affable Columbian providing directions to tourists on a train. On the steps of the Old Marylebone Town Hall in London, a man with black hair and olive skin stopped me, his eyes alight. Was I from Iran? I was not, and his eyes dulled. I was sorry to disappoint him. Occasionally people look at me with suspicion, as if I might steal something, or raise their voices when they speak to me, as if I am slow to understand. I have been mistaken for a waitress, a retail assistant, the nanny of my own blond child. Once, when a courier delivered a package to my office, his German shepherd dog barked ferociously at me through the van window. The dog had previously belonged to a security firm and was trained to bark at dark-skinned people walking near building sites.

Another unease is in deflecting the disquieting label "exotic." People intend it as a compliment, but it makes me squirm like a specimen about to be pinned under glass. If I am the exotic, then they are the usual, the standard, the rule.

In my twenties, while walking on a beach in Thailand, I was approached by a German man, who asked me, "How much?" I saw myself through his eyes: a slender woman in a sarong, my brown skin interpreted as a right to an exchange, a body for cash, subservience for power. I felt grubby, soiled by his view. I understood very directly then that whiteness could see, often did see, brown as *less than*.

Now I recognize it more frequently, more obviously. I live in America, but I was raised in New Zealand, which has its own layering of colonizer and colonized, migrants and people of the land, indigenous Māori, whites from England, Ireland, continental Europe, South Africa, Pacific peoples from Samoa, Tonga and Niue, Asians from India, Fiji, China, Hong Kong and Taiwan. In America, I haven't yet absorbed the local code whereby one knows one's place, but I've been here long enough to notice that it exists and that I sometimes tangle myself up in the semaphore. Unspoken and subtle markers manifest in body language, crossed arms, flickering eye contact, and a particular tone of voice, a light condescension—signaling that the speaker makes assumptions about status and intelligence. It is hard to prove prejudice or discrimination. How do I know? Do I imagine it?

Voices trail off when you join a group griping about Asians or Mexicans or Samoans or Māori or Indians, depending on the country you are in. These animals, these cockroaches are pushy / driving badly / not speaking English / living all together / writing signs in a foreign language / littering / shoplifting / mugging / breaching the border / taking our jobs / fucking our women. Nothing is said directly to you, unless you challenge a prevailing view and then you can't take a joke / are too politically corrrect / don't know that behind every stereotype is a truth.

Scrolling down the comments section of a blog or news article, I see what some folks say anonymously. I feel clammy and churny. They could be talking about me. I could be that animal.

It helps when I speak, because I have a New Zealand accent, and that is regarded as charming, and possibly English or South African or Australian. There is a pecking order of accents. In America, New Zealanders rank highly in this hierarchy, because we are a rare species, usually educated, employed and affluent, and most that live in the U.S. are white. Some people think New Zealand is situated next to England, or possibly attached to Australia; it clearly is not part of Latin America or Asia or any swath of lands imagined to produce only house cleaners and drug dealers. The status of accent hauls me back up the social rungs, and I'm embarrassed to admit that I prefer my perch.

Brown is often conflated with class: working class,

poor, the color of waiters, landscape gardeners, dishwashers, janitors, security guards. Of course there are brown pop stars, sports people, politicians, actors, and investment bankers—just not so many. At the college where I teach, some students tell me they have only had white teachers previously. The other brown and black teachers are, like me, likely to be adjuncts, or to work in areas where their darkness is related to the subject they teach. I don't know what to make of it when my friends and colleagues are kind and fair-minded people who despise racism, but seem powerless to change it.

I WANT TO be seen for what is inside, rather than being seen as my color. When trying to capture ideas about race, color, ethnicity, I am like my dog chasing his tail. Tomorrow I may think differently. Forgive me if my ideas shift as I grasp for the quicksilver of brown. Mutable brown.

I HAVE TWO sons, one fair, one dark. When the older boy was very young, we took baths together. His skin was satiny pale, his eyes cornflower, his ringlets strawberry blond. "What color are we?" I asked. "You are purple with green stripes and I am blue with orange spots," he responded. When he was a newborn, women asked how I knew he hadn't been swapped in the hospital. My heart swooped. "He was born at home," I replied. "He was the only baby there." We moved to Chicago when he was seven. He learned to introduce me to his friends in this way:

"This is my mom. I know she doesn't look like me, but she is my real mother."

When my second son was born, black-haired and olive-skinned, our midwife offered family counseling, as if there was something aberrant in the genetic deck. I was bemused, as my own family of origin resembled the bloom from a packet of wildflower seed, full of dazzling surprises in various shapes and colors. The wife of a colleague recently offered me a card for an organization catering to biracial families—I have heard it said that I have a biracial marriage. I have no idea which bits are bi- and which bits are multi-, and am floored that anyone outside my marriage is interested.

A student in my class said, vehemently, that he opposed biracial marriages. My mouth felt stuffed with cotton swabs. In the 1970s, when my white sister planned her marriage, her future in-laws were reluctant, because their potential grandchildren might "have a touch of the tar brush." But that was then. I thought we were beyond those fears.

A memory: my husband nicknamed our boys The Milky Bar Kid and Pixie Caramel, after candy bars popular in New Zealand. One is cream, the other brown. Both sweet.

My youngest son looks like me when I was a child, slim as a reed, lustrous chestnut hair glinting with red and gold from our Scottish forebears, rich brown eyes and long lashes, silky golden skin. I have fallen in love with my son's topaz glow, his nuggety tan in summer.

I worry about his brownness. He is lovely, funny, and sharp as a tack. It pains me that he may be categorized, diminished, or even hurt because of his tawny skin. I am watchful, alert to teachers passing him over, parents speaking carelessly, shopkeepers scrutinizing him as if he has stolen candy in his pocket, police seeing a criminality in him that isn't there. When a dark boy wearing a hoodie was shot dead, I warned my dark son not to wear his hood up. My pale son admonished me. Kids should wear what they want without fear, he said. I should ignore the stupidity, not reinforce it, he said. He doesn't understand my fear. I have never needed to warn my white-skinned boy about such dangers.

The color and shine of wood. Mahogany doors glowing in late afternoon sunlight. Boy's slender feet sliding across oak floors. Husband's guitars in ash, maple, spruce, and rosewood. The sycamore next to my bedroom, with its vitiligo-patched trunk, birches unfurling tan bark. Metal and earth. Rust peeling out from under old steel. Train tracks, Chicago brick warehouses, Frank Lloyd Wright terracotta, freshly worked soil in my spring garden. Birch wicker wrapped around a chrome chair. Old book spines in chestnut cabinet. Dappled pony skin chaise. Matching brindle hound dog lying next to the chaise. I am grateful for brown.

I MAY NOT want to be defined by brown, by my brownness, but I appreciate its nuance, its depth and complexity. I don't want to wear it, but I have warmed to it. I am not color-blind, nor do I wish to be. I like how I look, how my sons look. This is a part of who we are.

A memory: my boys and I, our summer legs curled together on the porch chaise, looking out onto the syca-more tree, our skin warm against one another's, dark tan, golden tan, pale clover honey.

ON AUTOIMMUNITY

WE WALKED IN a fog after 9/11. Everyone was overwhelmed. I know I was. People exhausted themselves, putting up flags and lighting candles, holding vigils and asking why anyone would attack America. They wanted to know how to secure the nation's borders, how to keep out trouble. A week later, anthrax killed five people. The government told us to seal our windows with plastic and duct tape so rogue spores, sent by a foreign enemy, couldn't penetrate and kill us. Years later, it appeared the threat came from inside.

I was in my own cloud, my borders porous and barely patrolled by a failing autoimmune system. My body turned on itself and I became a woman I no longer recognized.

THERE WAS BLOOD. One morning, I woke to crimson stains across the bed sheets and a boot polish-like crust under my fingernails. Menstruation lasted for weeks, not days. At first, I assumed it was a one-off event, an anomaly after a lifetime of regular, painless, easily containable, five-day periods, but the bleeding became clotty, ugly, and unpredictable. My mental fog grew thicker, denser. Dr. Setti, an internist at the nearby medical family practice, said I was anemic. She prescribed iron pills. I expected to be strengthened, to gain fortitude, but my margins weakened.

Susan Sontag said illness is *not* a metaphor, right after drawing one: "Everyone who is born holds dual citizenship, in the kingdom of the well and the kingdom of the sick." It is difficult for me to avoid making meaning through metaphor, at a time when my body seemed to mirror what was happening in the world.

MY HUSBAND AND I visited New Mexico for a film festival. Over breakfast with a group of philanthropists in a woman's home near the mountains of Albuquerque, blood seeped down my thighs, through my white skirt and pooled in the buttons of the dining chair cushion. The donors finished their fruit plates and drained their coffee mugs. Afraid to move, I sat glued in my mess, as droplets slid down the chair leg and into the pale carpet until the festival backers filed out.

My body's betrayal terrified me—the redness, the chunky pieces of jelly that tumbled out, pieces of my interior falling, out of control. What hemoglobin I had left spilled over; my cup could not contain all of me. My sons noticed droplets across the floor, smears on the towels, a crimson tide under the toilet seat, clots in the bowl. My then eight-year-old asked about the Australian-shaped stain on my bed's mattress. I told him it was sweat. Every time I visited the bathroom I feared death—imagining my essence leaking out, the children shaking my limp body on the cold white tiles. Never so much blood.

BACK I WENT to the doctor. She didn't test my blood, or examine my abdomen. This time, she diagnosed per-imenopause, the years when hormone levels shift and women experience changes in their menstrual cycle including periods irregular in timeliness, duration, and flow. And hot flashes. Hot flashes? No. It was a crisp, sunny start to fall and the leaves in my street were bare-ly tawny at the edges, but my feet felt painfully icy. I took hot showers to thaw them before bed. My flashes were strictly frigid. And no intercourse was going to get the blood flowing to them, because between the other blood, and the tiredness, and the lank hair invading our marital bed, and the iciness placed on my husband's leg to warm up, intercourse, social or sexual, was not a high priority.

My hair coiled around the shower drain. Tumble-weeds of it blew across the living room and gathered with the dust bunnies in corners and under tables. My husband complained that the pillow was matted with dark threads. I was too tired to style my hair, so it lay in a limp, thin blanket around my shoulders.

I was tired, always. Uncharacteristically, I fell asleep on the zebra sofa one afternoon with my boys wrestling like lion cubs on top of me, on my chest, on my belly. It was a heavy hurtling towards deep sleep, which I had only ever encountered in the early stage of pregnancy, when a woman can lunge in seconds from awake to a drugged-out, sleep-through-a-fire-drill slumber.

Moving is sapping, anyone knows that. Transporting two kids and a family's possessions across the globe from New Zealand required energy, which I had had in abundance. There, I chased my kids around our quarter-acre yard, worked out at the gym three times a week, climbed one hundred steps to my office most days, walked on the beach, and hiked up and down hills. In the uprooting, my body protested. So many boxes. Books, baby photographs, the blond curls from my son's first haircut, preschool finger paintings, a collection of Swedish hand-blown glass votives. All carried, box by box, up the steep stairs to our second-floor apartment. That would make anyone tired, wouldn't it? I had expected that sloughing off the banal—the routines of work and the obligations of extended family—would be invigorating, like a cold lap after a sauna, a salty scrub after the smooth. Instead, I experienced a slow slide into a deep, tepid pool that grew cold and thick, until I no longer had the will or strength to climb out. Was I depressed, I wondered? Maybe this was how women at home usually feel.

Maybe the move, maybe 9/11, maybe caring for children caused this malaise, a mental exile brought about by physical motion.

Out of body experiences overtook real body engagement. I accompanied my husband to a fancy gala in North

Chicago. Waking up strewn across a Mies van der Rohe chaise, I looked down from the ceiling at myself, all cinematic elegance in a red wool coat and high black boots against a marble floor.

In fact, I was a rumpled, clammy mess, splayed out and dissolving in and out of consciousness. During the second course of our meal, something in my chest began to flutter and cavort. My hands turned to liquid and my mouth went dry. I carefully folded my white linen napkin, told my husband I felt faint, and teetered out to the lobby where I passed out.

Maybe the waitstaff thought I was drunk. I dredged myself up from a dark horizon and begged a youth in a white apron to find my husband. He appeared as guests filtered out from dinner. Unaware of the danger, my husband eagerly introduced me to the president of his organization. I managed to prop myself on my elbows and shake an outstretched hand. It seems as strange to me now as it did then that no one called an ambulance, that my husband carried on as if nothing happened, that I fulfilled my social obligation to smile and greet my husband's boss from a horizontal position on a chaise. I was woozy and frightened, and checked in with my doctor again. She diagnosed SVT, sudden ventricular tachycardia. She said I may have a heart disorder which sometimes kills people, and sometimes recurs, but sometimes doesn't, and anyway, she wasn't sure.

No one around me seemed particularly alarmed. My

husband says now that he tried to keep stress levels down. He worried about the children. He feared that I might have a congenital heart condition. When he was a kid, he knew a boy who was discovered to have a "hole in his heart." The boy died.

I was afraid of what I didn't know, and of the person I had become. The endless winter and the children, cooped up inside for too long, were killing me. I was fragile, like the last shard of soap. I was the crazy, crying woman at the reception counter in the doctor's office, pleading for an appointment. It was March. I couldn't get an examination appointment until May.

"Honey, Dr. Setti's trying to get rid of her HMO patients. That's why she isn't making appointments," a nurse told me. HMO? I was used to New Zealand's government-funded health system; I didn't understand what she meant. Anyway, I had a PPO.

MY FRIENDS, A Colombian woman and her Argentinean husband, invited me to a party at their house. There was dancing and singing, empanadas and tequila, but I lay quietly on the couch. Someone filmed me. In the home video I look like a wraith.

Snow fell thickly as I left. I turned from my friends' driveway into the swirling silence. Orbs of blue-white light grew bigger directly before me as my car drifted on the slippery road. I realized I was driving on the left, not the right. Somehow in my drift, in the absence of color, I ended up in another country, on the wrong side of the road.

FOR SPRING BREAK I flew with my family to Mexico, into sunshine and hummingbirds and protests against the American invasion of Iraq—the "Shock and Awe" campaign. Cuernavaca, the city of eternal springs, was where Cortes had his summer palace. I swam in the pool and felt replenished by warmth and the bright colors of hibiscus and parrots. I climbed temples and walked miles up cobbled streets, feeling close to normal.

At dinner, peacocks strolled about the gardens of a grand old restaurant, shrieking like infants as we drank cocktails at dusk. We were with another family, whose parents lived in the city.

Wait before you drink a second margarita in Mexico.

MY BODY REBELLED against altitude and alcohol, or whatever sickness was sucking my tolerance for drink right into the television screen. One and a half margaritas were all it took to send the ceiling into a 78 rpm spin. My husband and kids hunkered down together in our quiet dark bedroom, while I sat upright in the children's adjoining bedroom, glowing in the psychedelic flicker of *Dora the Explorer*. I was unable to lie down for fear of spinning right out of the window into faraway brightness, sweating and heaving towards dawn.

I FOUND A new doctor, Dr. Reynes. He took blood tests, but struggled to find a plump vein. By the time he had finished, I had bruises down my arm and punctures on the top of my hand. They didn't make a tiny sting or a burn, but a throbbing hurt that made my eyes well. He sent me to a hospital technician who made me drink a gallon of water, and then put a probe inside me, checking for fibroids or cancer. I wanted to urinate so badly; my bladder felt like a kicked soccer ball.

There were questionnaires to fill out:

Does your skin itch? *Yes.*

Is your hair falling out? *Yes.*

Are you tired? *Yes.*

Do you have too much energy? *No.*

Do your eyes bulge? *No.*

Are your periods regular? *No.*

Are you constipated? *Not when I drink a lot of coffee.*

Have you gained or lost weight? *Gained.*

Do you have diarrhea? *Only when I drink too much coffee.*

Do you have palpitations? *Sometimes.*

Do you think of death? *Once a day, when it's time to get up.*

THE BUTTERFLY EFFECT describes when a small change at one particular place in a complex system has tremendous consequences. When Edward Lorenz made the term popular, he was thinking of chaos theory and meteorology, and the possible impact of an insect's wings on a hurricane. I, however, think of my pituitary gland, which anatomy books describe as butterfly-shaped. Its small disturbance caused a hurricane in my complex endocrine system and brought it crashing down.

The first medical scientist to describe the disease, in 1912, was Hashimoto Hakaru. The malady, known as *Struma lymphomatosa*, was renamed for him: Hashimoto's Thyroiditis. Dr. Hashimoto, who died of typhoid in 1934, also has a street named in his honor, at Kyushu University. The disease, which affects mainly women, is also known as chronic lymphocytic thyroiditis.

The pathology involves the immune system's destruction of the thyroid gland. Leukocytes, white blood cells, invade the live tissue as if it was a foreign body. As the organ dies, it loses its ability to produce thyroid hormone. The patient is said to have hypothyroidism. Symptoms may include paresthesia, myxedematous psychosis, bradycardia, tachycardia, fatigue, reactive hypoglycemia, memory loss, weight gain, hair loss, migraines, and cramps. The condition rarely resolves itself, but is treated with tablets of thyroid hormone, dessicated from pig glands or produced synthetically. If Hashimoto's Thyroiditis is untreated, it can lead to heart failure and death.

IT IS CURIOUS, how one's body—the vessel that both contains the "I" and *is* the "I"—can cannibalize itself. For a while, I felt like an indistinct replica of my former being, close to a shade or specter. I was undiminished in size—to the contrary, there is more of me now than there ever was before, the consequence of a slowed metabolism. I do not like that there is *more* of me, thirty pounds more. But I do like that there *is* me, still.

A chronic disorder, Hashimoto's has to be managed with regular checkups and blood tests. I have healed, by and large, and I no longer think of myself as diseased, although I still have dis-ease. Fluctuations in dosage or up-take of medication cause shifts in thyroid levels, and pre-dispose me to viruses and high cholesterol. Autoimmune disorders such as diabetes tend to cluster, so I count my steps and ration my calories, mindful of the enemies within. I try to keep a balance between vigilance and over-reaction. Again, I think of the warning against metaphor. The body is just the body. I shouldn't turn my illness into an allusion, but I can't help thinking my body is part of the culture, my divisions are artificial.

Sontag wrote that x-rays make the body "transparent to oneself." I have had my thyroid scanned and seen myself. I have also had my body scanned at the border, becoming transparent to TSA officials. I am not permitted to see that self. And just as an x-ray cannot reveal what occurs at a cellular level inside me, a TSA agent cannot see the intention in a traveler's mind, a worker cannot second-guess the future terrorism of a colleague, a parent cannot imagine their child as a serial killer.

Sometimes a nightmare wakes me, panting, with the sheet wrapped around my foot and the pillow on the floor. A cataclysm, perhaps an earthquake or tornado, has destroyed the country's infrastructure. I have run out of medicine and cannot access further supplies. Without my thyroid hormone, I fear my blood will pool around me, my hair will fall away, my heart will stop beating. We cannot know where and when our defenses will be breached, in our culture, in our natures. We have long feared what would come from the outside; we are slower to understand the dangers within.

UNRAVELING

I DISTURBED A nest of baby rabbits under the catmint as I hacked back the dead sprawl. Something moved under my loppers. Five nestlings, each the size of a small teacup, curled into each other, wrapped in a tender blanket of down shed from their mother. Eyes closed, mewling, wriggling in my grasp. I wanted to protect them. I wanted to kill them.

Baby rabbits, or kits as they are known, have no smell, apparently so predators don't detect them. Now they would smell of me. Their mother would reject them because of their new sweaty-hand-and-dank-garden-glove scent. I felt for this sweet brood, but turned instead to my garden. This is where I coaxed blue campanula to come back after winter, and tried to keep order among the reckless bee balm and catmint. A mother rabbit, a doe, can birth six litters in a season. I didn't want them ransacking my garden, nibbling my asters to stubs, disrupting the line of creeping phlox by chewing them ragged. Nor did I want my dog to find sport in them, playing a macabre game with a score tallied in limp bodies. I gave the brood to our neighbors, who passed them along the block to Illinois Sam, an obsessive collector of rodents and other beasts. Motherless, those thumpers died, but at least not on my watch.

LATER, IN SUMMER, I found a lone kit, wet from my hound's mouth, lying damaged on the lawn, roaring silently. His mouth stretched wide, tiny see-through teeth vibrating. He made me think of Edvard Munch's "The Scream," the image that stares out from dorm room posters and kitchen towels and mouse pads, reminding us that human distress can spiral out for eternity. It's called "Skrik" in Danish, capturing the moment in a life when raw pain prevails.

I filmed my tiny screamer on my phone, thinking it might be useful for some later project, as a record of anguish. I filmed as he ran out of shriek, until his mouth barely quivered ajar. He no longer had strength to raise his head from the grass. His crying slowly lost its desperation, trailing into a soundless mew. Did he cry for his mother? Was she hiding under the wild mess of golden rod and dock by the garage, or watching from a burrow beneath the deck? I knelt beside him, a surrogate parent offering comfort by being present. As if a parent's presence alone could be enough. A parent of any species. In this case, a human mother with a camera, recording his torment. Watching him, I felt both invested in his suffering and detached. Sympathy and cool voyeurism coiled together. I shivered.

The sun blared directly above. Steamy. Sweat trailed into my eyes, down my arm onto my camera, and still I shot my little film. Mid-shot. His dappled fur was slicked flat and shimmered with dog slobber, but his body was perfect and unpunctured. Close up. A fly settled on his eye. Extreme close-up. How quickly the shiny jet bead turned dull, its intensity clouding opaque. I felt a slight guilty sourness for observing his life spool away in the hot sun, for not thinking him worth rescuing, but he was a wild thing, a pest, not my offspring, not a creature I valued. I put his body in a Jewel-Osco bag and tossed him in the brown bin.

WHAT KIND OF real mother would film the death of a child? A mother like me would photograph her son on the cusp of dying. I did, when my now almost grown firstborn was a baby. I was an attentive enough mother. I did some of the "right" things according to the cultural norms of mothers I knew in New Zealand, where my son was born. I did not drink alcohol or coffee or eat soft cheeses when I was pregnant. I birthed at home, nursed on demand, used cloth diapers, and introduced solid foods according to a pediatric calendar. I let him do things that were not prescribed: eat dirt from the flower pot, scoot naked around the garden, and look at colorful books fastened with clothes pegs to the side of his stroller. He was a happy, plump baby. When he got a cough, I took him to the doctor, three times, and then to the hospital. There, my son, barely breathing, convulsed with fever and pneumonia. In the photograph, he is behind bars, encaged by a high-sided hospital bed, his pallid little body wearing a diaper, a drip, and an oxygen tube. I want to reach in and touch him, make sure his flesh is still warm and his chest is still rising and falling. Did I photograph my baby to record his anguish, or as a totem to his health? The image preserves a moment faded by sleepless nights and time, reconstructed as a memory in the slip-in plastic envelope of the photo album. It speaks to the isolation of illness, a solitary infant sequestered from his family. My boy's tiny hand on a book shaped like a train. The grinning face of his Humpty Dumpty doll. White hospital sheets creased sharply in the center. Photograph has become memory, a past so examined that the album covers have loosened and are pulling away.

Not too long ago, a colleague lost her two-year-old grandson from pneumonia. His parents had done the "right" thing in taking him to the hospital, but the child was sent home and did not wake. I felt sorrow for that family, and a wash of relief that my boy survived his pneumonia, as well as the thigh impaled by a bike peg, the concussion, the appendicitis, the knee surgery, the ear surgery, and the varieties of physical and emotional anguish over the years from which no amount of vigilance could protect him.

Good fortune can turn on a dime. Those we nurture so carefully can dissolve from our grasp, no matter how tenderly we blanket them. The downy cradle can unravel. We humans are part of the natural web, after all, no matter how we try to disengage. Natural order is unlike the cosseted plants in my garden, the intentional linearity of blues, whites, and greens. Instead, its unpredictable beauty tangles, entraps, erupts, chokes, and frequently kills. My boy survived. The hospital photograph remains in my album, as a failed *memento mori*. I wear a pendant of charms that I fondle like a rosary: a silver dove, a garnet heart, and a skull threaded with tiny pearls. I do remember death, and I hope that in remembering, I am somehow protected from its disorder, or at least, that my loved ones will be safe.

MY NEIGHBOR HAS a different relationship to the mess of life. Illinois Sam invites chaos into his parlor, revels in it. He cultivates the persona of a rebel. Maybe that's how he attempts to keep real destruction at arm's length. But when I looked closer, I see a tangle of organization and disorder, care and neglect, nurture and murder, not so dissimilar to my own arrangement with reality.

We have a lot of wildlife on our block, because of Sam. He loves squirrels. One day I counted twenty scampering on the grassy parkway in front of our houses. I was intrigued that he could have such a heart for them. He cares for them, while I loathe them. The squirrels like Illinois Sam. He feeds them peanuts in their shells. He used to feed them birdseed. The rats, too, loved Sam back then. They would dine in his back yard, then slink to our pond for a drink. In winter I would see their dark forms skulking across the snowy lawn and disappearing under our back deck. Their numbers increased, until Sam started killing them with his BB gun. One day, he shot eight. He protected the squirrels like his own, yet he stalked the rats that he attracted. Not all animals have the same value. He watched the rats in his sights for hours. Then he pulled the trigger, again and again. The capacity for tenderness and death are wrapped tightly within us; the rescuer capable of nurturing and hanging on to life—or discarding it.

The neighborhood tolerated Illinois Sam and liked him well enough. He was a quirky, humorous guy. He seemed to fancy himself a blow-stuff-up, shoot-'em-up, good for a drink and a story guy. The kind of guy it would be fun to go hunting with at his Tennessee cabin, if you had a bottle of Jack and liked hunting and dynamiting things. Or at least, the neighbors and I acted as though that would be fun, when he told us his stories. In reality, we were a bunch of office-paled professionals whose experience with explosives was limited to action movies. Our lives were quietly controlled. We admired each other's ambitions and gardens and homes, but enquired little about any decay in the façades.

Sam wore a taxidermied squirrel on his shoulder to our block party. I thought it was real. He sat around the fire and spun tales about how back in the day when he went to the local high school, the students had to swim naked. First, the boys had to sprint through a shower on the floor, spraying icy water into their nether regions. He told us how the shock made their scrotums shrivel and their penises shrink, which is about when the block-party ladies from the fancy big houses up the street drifted away from the brazier to check on their children dismembering pumpkins, and the men sifted across to the beer cooler to talk property taxes and football.

Illinois Sam definitely "added character to the block," the euphemism people use when an individual almost conforms to social norms, but misses the mark. He added Republican leanings to a street of Democrats, drunkenness to conventional daytime sobriety, a hillbilly house behind a groomed frontage. His front garden was photographed for the local newspaper. He grew a neat row of hostas and impatiens along the path to his porch and blew the fallen leaves off his lawn every day, several times a day, even in summer, when leaves don't fall regularly. In the photograph you see the hostas and the impatiens, the tidy lawn. You see Sam with his ponytail and his Grateful Dead t-shirt, a hose in one hand and a beer can in the other, at ten in the morning. *Nunc est bibendum.* Now is the time to drink.

I came to both detest and pity him. He regaled me about gun rights and emailed me birther conspiracies about the nation's first black president. His life, like others around us, was on the skids, and for that I was sorry. I sympathized with his slide. Maybe, as the structure of his life came apart, he focused on what he could influence—sustaining creatures smaller than him. Still, I was riled that I had to pay to replace the soffits on my house when the squirrels chewed them apart. Sam fed them in all seasons, boosting their numbers and attracting rats. The rats made burrows in our yard. Our dog choked on a peanut meant for the squirrels. The squirrels bred until the neighborhood yards were overrun and the pear tree was stripped of fruit. They lived in his house. They were family. I don't know what his wife thought. The couple's own children had grown up, and moved out, and back, and next door, never far, but clearly the urge to nurture compelled Sam to keep the wild things unusually close.

We try to look after what is in our circle of care, what we think we can control, when all that is around us spirals into chaos. I really don't understand how the Dow falls, or what derivatives are, or how corporations can shed millions of workers in a day. The language of recession is hollow—it reveals nothing of the work of merely holding on, of pretending that life is the same.

Once, Sam said hello to me with a squirrel on his shoulder. I assumed it was stuffed, until it jumped on his head. Beyond the tamed front garden patch, unruly yews wound across the porch and over the crawl space piled with glinting beer cans, where rabbits, rats, and squirrels dart. The side of his house visible from ours was covered in creeper, concealing the windows and crawling along the gutters, peeling paint from the siding and slowing tearing tarpaper from the places where the boards have rotted off.

The squirrels sat on the roof, gnawing at the eaves.

There were so many, spreading out and chewing into our attic and the cavities above my family's beds. We heard them scratching and mating in the night, and saw them leaping from fresh holes in our new soffits into the trees and onto the power lines.

They were among us. In our bedrooms, scampering across the white linen and up between the windows. In our office, waiting silently for us at dawn. In the glasses cupboard, smashing up champagne flutes as though they were at a Greek wedding. We didn't invite them. We never knew how they got in. It's a mistake to think wild things can be tamed, just as we are mistaken if we think protection is fully in our realm.

Illinois Sam and his wife put their house on the market. Apparently, they hadn't paid their mortgage or property taxes in years, so foreclosure was likely. The Great Recession bit hard into our neighborhood. It seemed that some people clung to the artifice of order, mulching their parkway trees and keeping their boxwood hedges trimmed, but beyond the screen doors, they quietly panicked about their retirement savings, their mortgages, employment hopes, and their kids' college funds. We could smell the wildness beyond the parkway. The control we all thought we had gave way to quiet despair. Houses went unpainted for longer, holiday decorations seemed sparser, the landscaping crews worked less frequently, while the suitcases and piles of furniture sitting untended outside emptied apartments became more frequent. There were several houses for sale on our leafy block of mainly Victorians, Italianates, and Painted Ladies. The owner of the blue two-flat sold because she was addicted to prescription painkillers. The brick house and its coach house were subject to a short sale after the owner hung himself and was found by his son, who had just finished high school.

There was a sense of middle and working class townsfolk barely keeping it together, a spiraling out, in the way our parkway maples sent their seeds helicoptering down in unexpected gusts. My family remained secure enough in health and work, but it all seemed more fragile. Amid anxious nights, I wondered how to pay the mortgage if my husband lost his solid job, how to cover health costs when the insurance vanished. What would I do if he died? In dreams, I rehearsed for disaster. By day, I tended my garden. I could contain that, at least.

My eldest son, a high school senior, began his college search. I wanted to contain him, but I knew that foot binding would be fruitless. All of the latent worries I had pushed down since he was a baby started boiling up to my hot surface. I was afraid of the fragility within him, and all the frightening possibilities of the world. They were possibilities that I was oblivious to in the thirty-four years before I had him, when life seemed perennially in bloom and opportunities boundless. Now I wanted strangers to be kind to him, as they were those nights in the hospital when he struggled for breath and whimpered for me. He did not know my catalogue of fears and I did not tell him:

the sophomore throttled by a tie, the freshman impaled in a car crash, the cousin's blood clot, the cousin's strep-infected boil, my own line-up of college friends ruined by drugs, accidents, illness, love, unravelings.

Instead I propelled him forward, made him clean his room, schedule his own appointments, open a bank account, wash his laundry—as if happy independence could be guaranteed by white and dark laundry piles and a made bed. I was excited for his freedom and wanted him unfettered, but I knew that his departure would be a sort of mini-death. I wonder, now: what will be left of these boys in my life?

AMERICA SEEMS LARGE, the world larger, and I know that children sprawl out wide, as my own mother discovered, and countless mothers of immigrants, travelers and pioneers in covered wagons have experienced since the first great migrations reverberated with their children's absence. Like the rabbits in my yard, parents closely watch their helpless young, and then all but cast them to fate or luck, watching nervously from the hedgerows to see if they thrive.

Illinois Sam's unraveling sped up after his mother died. He'd lost his job when arthritis clawed his hands and he'd lost his market value. Watching out for his old mother had kept him stitched together, in a reversal of parenting roles. After her death, he focused his watchfulness into squirrels and lawn. He strode up and down the line of hostas in his yard, blowing leaves and drinking beer at all hours. I don't know where those leaves came from, so thick and fast, and well before fall. He tinkered endlessly on unfinished and unfathomable house projects, moving boxes and throwing junk in the alley. His wife moved first. Then Sam, officially, though he came back every few days. He sat with his legs stretched down the porch steps, chatting to his extended family of grey squirrels.

My house became quieter. My growing boys spent more time away as the open road shimmered in the distance. One night in winter the icicles hanging off the eaves glowed red and orange. I rushed to the window and saw a bonfire on the chilled white waste of Sam's back yard. Flames surged up toward the moonlit spire of St. Edmund's cathedral across the alley. Three snowy nights in a row, I saw Sam lurching tipsily from the house, throwing his leftover junk into the pit.

That spring, I spent my first night alone at home for years. I'd imagined calm as merely the absence of noise—balls thudding into the basement walls, wrestling matches, bickering, sniffing, and cracking of knuckles. There would be no dirty socks peeled off by the sofa, shoes and backpacks dispersed inside the front door, or peanut butter congealing on un-rinsed knives in the kitchen sink. But the moment I had longed for seemed silent and hollow, and I was restless until the clatter of my children and husband returned.

My son and I forged on with college applications and

financial forms, and looked at websites showing distant campuses with sun and youth, ivy growing on old stone, and sundials inscribed *Ultima Forsan*, "Perhaps the last," and *Vulnerant Omnes*, "They all wound," and *Ultima Necat*, "The last kills." I didn't want to think of a last hour, or what could wound or kill, or who might be watching, so I pushed my fears back down again and sought order in my garden.

THE BANK OWNS Sam's house now. A realtor told us it was a "teardown," that the woodwork is all chewed up inside. Ferns and rabbits overtook the front garden. There was a ferret on the loose in the bedroom, squirrels sat inside on the sofa, and rodent feces trailed throughout the house. Sam had carefully built a bathroom right in the middle of the living room, but hadn't repaired the chew holes in the upstairs bedrooms, so green tendrils crept down the plasterboard and across the floors. The outside was coming in relentlessly. Creepers and squirrels know no boundaries if you give them the chance. Even when you try to control them.

THREE OF THE rose bushes I planted in my garden last fall survived the snowy winter, but have been stripped of their spring leaves. My husband erected fortresses of plastic fencing around them to save them from the latest batch of rabbits. I see my new phlox plants are nude, their pink flowers erased overnight. I'm furious. As I step off the back deck, I see a tiny dappled rabbit cowering, quiv-ering. My scalp tingles with rage, and I look around for a weapon. I reach for a solar light embedded in the lawn, imagining its javelin-like end spearing the rabbit. But the creature dives under the deck and is gone.

BEQUEATHED

RUPTURING

THE CITY OF my youth is ruptured, warped, and broken. My brother is dead. It is what it is, I say, with fingernails-on-chalkboard insouciance. Ring-of-fire broken. Cancer-broken. At once.

IN ONE SLOWLY seeping week in February 2011, an earthquake in the southern New Zealand city of Christchurch killed 185 people, destroyed one hundred and fifty thousand homes and churned up four hundred thousand tonnes of liquid silt. Around the same time, my brother was diagnosed with terminal cancer. The quake shot out tatters of sibling something—guilt, duty, an expectation of sisterhood? This is no Hansel and Gretel tale where siblings help each other survive the big bad witch. Rather, this sister stood on the sidelines and watched ineffectually while the brother was devoured by malignance. There was no trail of breadcrumbs.

My homeland Aotearoa, land of the long white cloud, New Zealand, hovers over a seam in the Earth's unstable crust. Fault lines rebel often, knocking books off shelves and scattering cups in cupboards. A primal landscape hisses and steams, throwing rocks and ash from volcanoes, shuddering and groaning to relieve the pressure.

Every hundred years or so, it rages deeply, raining fire or rising up on itself. This time a sharp quake thrust up the sea floor and sliced apart my old city. It folded roofs and walls like some terrible origami, hurled bricks, devoured people, and rumbled through the city's mellow lunchtime hum.

MY BROTHER WAS there, somewhere.

CHRISTCHURCH SITS ON the edge of the South Island of the Shaky Isles. Flanked by alps formed by shifting plates, Christchurch faces the South Pacific Ocean, in the Southern Hemisphere, beneath the Southern Cross constellation. Here hurricanes cycle clockwise and you drive on the left side of the road. The beach undulates in summer heat while blizzards cross the United States, and temperatures soar in Celsius rather than Fahrenheit. The sun rises seventeen hours before it shines in Chicago, where I live.

My brother lived there most of his life. His was a life arrested early; he was strangled by his umbilical cord, a tragedy that slowed the flow of oxygen to his brain. Hypoxia kills cells, atrophies cognition, and interrupts neurotransmitters, including acetylcholine, which memory depends on. I don't know the full details. I hadn't thought to ask anyone for information, maybe because I was ten years younger than him. I was the baby of the family. He lived at home until I was born, then he was moved to an institution, and later to a group home, so I never knew him the way I knew my other siblings. He wasn't around to shove dirty socks in my face and make me smell them, to teach me how to pass a rugby ball, to tie my shoelaces or braid my hair. It seemed too late by the time I was an adult to ask my mother to tell me all the things I didn't know about him—did he like fudge, what was his favorite color, why did he go away?

I last visited my brother when I was eight. The journey seemed interminable. We drove through the city and past farms for ten miles, then turned down an avenue of dark tall trees, to Templeton Hospital and Training Center. I visualize a Gothic asylum, with brick towers and barred windows, but I'm pretty sure that's my imagination. I remember the blue and white knitted dress I wore. Stripes snaked up and down the skirt, riding the pleats so carefully made by my mother. The soft lambs' wool was the dark blue of Delft china, soothing to stroke and rub between my little fingers. I longed to be at home, listening to my mother's knitting needles clack in time with her mantra, "knit one, purl one, knit two together."

I didn't look at my brother because I was afraid, but I can't pinpoint why he frightened me. Did *he*—or did my memories of cinema hunchbacks and storybook characters—do that work for me? In photographs taken when he was a child, he seems a sweet, smiling boy, with heavy-lidded eyes and an overbite. As an adult, he appears with his head ducked down, with apple cheeks and a broad smile.

I was frightened of him for the same reasons that cause children to fear their inky windows at night or the lurking monsters in their shadowy closets—the neck-prickle of the unknown. I was shy and terrified and very small in that big place, the size of Bluebeard's castle. I boarded it up with my recurring dreams.

The health board eventually bulldozed Templeton and moved the residents into smaller homes. My brother stayed in Christchurch, and I returned years later as a university student. I didn't visit him, or think of him then. I moved far away. I grew up and never visited him when I went to Christchurch on business trips or passed through on vacation. I didn't visit when I wrote speeches about intellectually disabled people for a government minister in charge of social welfare. I didn't visit when I did public policy work for an agency working for people with disabilities. He was somewhere in my mind when I wrote about the policy of deinstitutionalization, jargon not sympathetic to brother.

I read stories about men and women who had spent lives behind walls, far from families, shadowed from potential, sequestered for convenience, misunderstanding or fear. My job was to persuade the Minister's constituents that it would be a good thing to close institutions and let intellectually impaired people live in the community. A government review uncovered institutional horrors: abuse, lack of dignity, Dickensian living conditions, and social exclusion. I wrote about how we know so much more now, how neurology, education and community support make it possible for people with intellectual disabilities to live with their families, in group homes, to work, to be normal. The idea of my brother helped inform me, but I did nothing to liberate him from the corner of my mind.

Today, little children of all abilities go to school together and skin their knees together and poke at dead creatures on the playground together and fidget in the same classrooms together. They don't see difference in the way I once did. I didn't go to school with my brother, or live with him, or know anyone like him. The State became his family.

WHEN AN EARLIER bigger earthquake, 7.1 on the Richter scale, hit the city five months earlier, it shunted the land sideways. No one was killed. It damaged my brother's house in the city center, so he and his roommates were moved to a rambling villa with a wrap-around porch in a pastoral village to the north. That was when he was diagnosed with diffuse large B-cell lymphoma, a cancer crawling through his blood. For the first time, after so many years and so much distance, I was called upon to be some sort of a sister to him. The best I could manage was to research and compile a list of questions for my family to ask the oncologist, and mail some Cubs and White Sox caps with a letter explaining: "I am your sister. You probably don't remember me . . ."

The next major rupture measured only 6.3 on the Richter, but it was six miles under the earth's surface and less than a mile from the city, under Lyttelton Harbor. It accelerated vertically, not horizontally, with almost twice the force of gravity. It destroyed Christchurch's center. As news spread onto television screens and computers and rescue teams crawled over wreckage, the moments warped as if caught in a strobe, a flickering, puddling mirage. I was captivated by the screen, sneaking moments and hours to search the rubble-strewn streets for faces and places from my past. Glommed to the computer's news feed, I saw shocked workers with bloodied faces and torn suits stumbling from twisted structures. Black dust plumed from a central business district reduced to rubble. The Catholic Basilica's front was ripped off, exposing its naked interior. Cliffs and boulders rumbled onto homes. I barely recognized the place. It was a media creation, not my city. When I last visited, the city had an ambling, faux English charm. I wandered along the Avon River, with its weeping willows and punters, and ambled up avenues lined with chestnuts and poplars.

I DIDN'T KNOW where my brother was for two days. I hoped he wasn't too frightened. I worried about this childlike man being afraid and not finding anyone to comfort him. He was working in a sheltered workshop, making baskets and doilies. That isn't a stereotype. That is what semi-institutionalized people often do for employment. I imagined him and his colleagues trapped and bleeding amidst tumbled bricks and straw strewn from shattered baskets. I saw him confused in the dark with no power and no one coming to save him. For a long night and half a day, I waited for news of him. Between confusion, disintegration, and time difference, it took a relay of phone calls from his caregivers to my family to me to let me know he was alive and somewhat safe.

I WEPT FOR Christchurch, not for my ill brother.

I wept for the nostalgia of childhood, of a warm home with my mother and the three siblings I was close to. It was easier to contemplate the city and its destruction, the deaths of strangers, rather than the demise of my own flesh and blood.

THAT WEEK, WE found that my brother had fresh tumors. Chemo shrank the old ones, but didn't arrest new growth. We had to decide on palliative radiation. We had to decide if he was to be moved from Christchurch to Wellington, near my middle sister and my mother, away from aftershocks.

My mother said no. My sister suggested my mother wanted him to die. Maybe she did. She feared that she would die before him, and what would happen then? She wanted him to stay where he was comfortable, close to his oncology team, to his caregivers, his surrogate family.

Life cannot be the same again when all that is known has been heaved up. Imagining this destruction leaves me gasping. There's a name for this distress. Environmental philosopher Glenn Albrecht calls it solastalgia.

> Caused by the loss of, or inability to derive, solace connected to the present state of one's home environment. Solastalgia exists when there is recognition that the place where one resides and that one loves is under assault (physical desolation). It can be contrasted to the spatial and temporal dislocation and dispossession experienced as nostalgia.

LOSS OF PLACE, loss of brother—they blur together. The famous Cathedral tower in the city center toppled when the earth bucked beneath it, its foundation skewed and shattered. It is the icon of postcards and calendars, meeting place of locals, tourist highlight and rock of the city's British colonial heritage. I had walked by it countless times. Now the Gothic spire sprawled across the paving stones. The leopards and lion on the coat of arms inside came from Christ Church in Oxford, England, a reminder of Christchurch's beginnings as a British colonial settlement. It was New Zealand's first city. I don't think I knew this before it fell, but now I clung to this fact as a talisman, as if the connection to heritage could keep my own family mortar from crumbling. Woven tukutuku panels, crosses of flax and leather threaded onto rimu wood, show Roimata, the splashing of tears, Poutama, the stairway to Heaven, and a proverb that says in Māori:

> *He aha te mea nui?*
> *He tangata, He tangata, He tangata*
> *What is the most important thing in life?*
> *It is people, people, people.*

I am unsure if I ever actually attended a service in the Cathedral. Does it just seem that way because the image was replayed over and over? Outside, the cobbled Cathedral Square of my childhood is now grave to steeple. I should think of my people, not just any people, but the universal is somehow easier to confront than personal failing. The more distant, the safer to let emotions bubble to the surface.

HUMAN HISTORY IS layered up in these plains. Long ago, Te Waka Orurea, one of the first Māori canoes, carried adventurers across the Pacific to these plains, then French whalers and British settlers.

> *He taonga nō te whenua me hoki anō ki te whenua*
> *What is given by the land should return to the land.*

Whenua: land, country, ground. It also means afterbirth, placenta. In New Zealand Māori tradition, a baby's afterbirth is buried, forming an irrevocable tie to the land. My sons' placentas are both buried in Aotearoa, one under an apple tree, one under a nikau palm. *Whanau,* related to *whenua*, is the word for *family*. This is important to me.

Sediment upon sediment. The wise man built his house upon a rock, and the wise man's house stood firm, but the foolish man built his house upon the sand, which turned out to be a rather bad idea in this city. It is a bad idea for people to construct their families on uncertain foundations, but we risk it anyway. In the earthquake, the sediment liquefied a grey, stinking ooze that killed plants and small animals.

I scraped away at my memory and realized I didn't like living in that city much anyway. When my family lived there, my father died. We moved away and onto reconfigured, reinvented lives. I returned briefly for a year of college, and then transferred to another city.

NOT SO LONG ago in Chicago, I took my young son to a drum recital in a musty meeting room at a local church. After a dozen boys and girls had beaten their way through Led Zeppelin and Nirvana solos, a young man played "Freedom Train" on the piano. His family was as proud as any family. The man clearly had an intellectual disability, and as he belted out "making us feel proud and true," I wept, my face turned down so no one could see. Perhaps if my brother grew up now, he would be celebrated for his abilities. It really doesn't matter if someone hoots and shouts while playing the piano, as long as they get to experience it. It won't frighten the children.

After my brother's death, my sister was given a report about him. It contained inaccuracies, crossings-out, white-outs, black-outs. His diagnosis was not as clear as we thought. No one was really sure what the cause was, whether it was hypoxia or autism. It saddened me that he was born when so little was known and therapies were inadequate. It seemed that if he had been born in a later decade, he might have stayed at home with his family.

I WATCHED AMATEUR videos of Christchurch that showed the places that television cameras hadn't captured. I saw a claggy surge of sediment power through a forest, an alluvial flood full of liquefaction forcing a new watercourse where no river had been before. Unruly sediment dislodged graves and uncovered secrets and scars. Most people stayed to rebuild their homes and businesses. Thousands left the city. The one hundred and eighty-five dead were buried.

My brother Robin—I should name him—died in the summer, at his home, peacefully. My sister stroked his hair and whispered to him as he slid away. She organized blue balloons. My eldest sister and I, both far away, found poems for his service. I imagined I would visit my brother, sometime, when the dust settled, when the Christchurch silt stabilized, when his dust had been cast into the Canterbury breeze.

A FEW MONTHS ago, during a quick trip to New Zealand, I stayed at my sister's house in Wellington. On a desk by a window overlooking the harbor, sat a small white rectangular plastic box. I peered closely at the printed label— my brother's ashes. I hadn't known they were there; it seemed hilarious and absurd that they were. I had imagined an elegiac farewell, to put things right, but this was distinctly unpoetic. It felt like knocking at a colleague's door too early in the morning and finding him in a bathrobe and bed socks. I backed off laughing, uttered no poignant words, made no gesture. For a moment we had been close to each other, as siblings sometimes are.

BLOOMING FOR
DESERVING EYES

Gardening is a good defense against memory, for it is all in the future.
— GERMAINE GREER

NARROW WATER, FRANCOISE Juranville, Madame Alice Garnier, Peace, Cardinal de Richelieu, Fourth of July, Constance Spry, Albertine—this is the music of my mother's roses. I photograph blooms for my mother. Whenever I travel, I send her rose mementos, photographs, postcards, soap, creams, perfume, tisanes, scarves, dried petals, syrup, trinkets. I made my son clamber over a neatly trimmed box hedge in Florence's Boboli Gardens to take the Tuscan shot, a pale pink bud framed by distant yew trees and an olive grove. I look through my albums and see a record of my mother traveling with me. She visited India as an infant and stayed home thereafter, but I like to think I can take the world to her—rosehips clustered outside an old pharmacy, a red rambler braided over a gate in Istanbul or a geyser of frothy Rosa mulliganii in Sissinghurst's white garden.

When I was a teenager, we could not be in the same room together without arguing—to shave legs or not to shave, how short to wear shorts, what time to come home. We argued into adulthood—to swaddle the newborn or leave unwrapped, to feed on demand or by schedule, which political party to support, to believe or dispense with God. Now, we have safe ground, united by our gardens in their opposite seasons. My russet chrysanthemums light up my fall garden. Her pastel primroses are out. My clematis browned in the heavy rains. I have cardinals singing from the burning bush. She has a tui calling in her kōwhai. While I wonder if my red climbing rose will survive this year's snow, my mother's roses are just budding on the other side of the world. "I picked three red flowers from the fence today. Crimson Conquest, grown from a cutting," she tells me when I call. "There's a lovely old fashioned tea rose, creamy white with a blush."

She gardened all through my childhood, in the many houses we moved to. Digging around the raspberry bushes, staking delphiniums, watering poppies, pruning roses, training a climber along a fence, potting up cuttings snipped from friend's bushes or pilfered on neighborhood walks. A lonely girl whose parents died when she was young, my mother dreamed of a rose-covered cottage. When she was old enough, she exiled herself from her hometown, fled from her unhappy past, and dug, spliced, divided, rooted, and seeded a more creative future. Old roses, heritage and historic, are her passion. She has grown herself a new heritage. I carry my mother with me and recall Alice Walker's poem "The Nature of this Flower is to Bloom":

> *Rebellious. Living.*
> *Against the Elemental Crush.*

A Song of Color
Blooming
For Deserving Eyes.
Blooming Gloriously
For its Self.

ON THEFT

IF YOU STEAL a frozen chicken, do not put it under your arm. Frozenness numbs your armpit. You cease to understand the boundaries of the bird. Where are you in relation to the frozen carcass? How far does your numbness extend? It becomes difficult to feel anything. My advice is not to steal. My advice is to trace your icy path back to your feelings.

WHEN YOU TEACH college freshmen, you hear many stories. The joys bubble up often, a sparkly scarf, new winter boots, new friendships; and the sadnesses, which they frequently try to bury, show up in the middle of things—love affairs broken, opportunities scuppered, dear ones lost.

Students are led to believe that freshman year is about beginnings, so the endings when they come, are unexpected and surprising. Ended affairs, friendships and the lives of loved ones often creep through the semester. They sometimes collapse in the students' pages, a graveyard of bleached bones amid the type.

I, TOO, WAS unprepared for endings the year I was a freshman, but they came anyway. The year was full of giddy fun and hilarity; the ridiculous laughter that comes with being a teenager still. Also, that year, my mother was divorced from her second husband. She crashed her car and nearly killed herself. My boyfriend left me when he got another girl pregnant. I lost two jobs. My roommate Stella's mother died. What do you do with all of that, when you are eighteen, living away from home for the first time?

STELLA HAD OPALESCENT skin and strawberry blonde hair dyed the color of flames. She wore thick eyeliner and a don't-fuck-with-me sneer, fishnets, and black industrial boots. Staunch. It was her idea to leave our dorm and look for a house off campus. We found a drafty wooden Victorian occupied by a guy we came to call Krazy Ken. He was ten to thirty years older than us—his uncombed long hair and wild beard made it hard to pin down—and looked like a triad of Lord Byron, Tommy Chong, and Keith Richards. Ken grew pot for a living, as in pounds of it in remote plantations. He told us he was a hunter and we believed him—it turned out his *true* prey were my friends, whom he conscripted to be his sales staff on campus. Faye, his girlfriend, was a casualty of angel dust and too much Jefferson Airplane. Lacking insulation or double windows, our house was always cold and damp, and smelled of pot and Ken's wet wool socks drying on a rack by the living room fire. We thought we had stepped into *real* adulthood.

To pay rent, we worked in a Swiss restaurant owned by a Dutchman, Hank Hoof. He ran his names together, and with his accent he said his name like "handcuff," in keeping with his porn-y choice of waitress uniforms. I wore a short orange dirndl—a skirt with suspenders—and a white blouse edged in rickrack braid. I was an unlikely Swiss Miss, with my brown skin and dark hair.

When the place first opened, people used to line up down the street to get in, so I was told, but it had long passed its heyday. The window boxes were chipped, the wooden chalet framing crumbling, and the cuckoo in the clock no longer appeared. One night there was a single customer, as in *one* customer. He was a regular, who came several times a week for roast beef and gravy and maybe a flash of my thigh beneath the micro dirndl. I took his order, but forgot to pass it to the kitchen. An hour later, he was still patiently waiting for his meal.

I THINK OF this when my first year students forget to turn in essays. There was certainly something about being eighteen that made basic tasks slip from *my* grasp. I lost the waitressing job. It was the second loss; I had previously failed at house painting. I once tipped a full pot of exterior matte white from the top of my ladder while painting an old guy's house. It flew through the open front door and up the hallway. I crawled on my hands and knees across a carpet woven with vines and peonies, blotting and mopping with a cotton rag. I willed the old guy to look the other way as he chatted to his friend in the adjacent living room. I hoped the bright white splotches would look like flowers, but I was not asked back.

STELLA'S MOM'S CANCER returned and burrowed into her spine, ten years after it appeared in her breast. Stella and I hitchhiked fourteen hours to visit her in the hospital. She was lying in bed, strapped up in a traction device to relieve the pressure on her back. Her conversation slid out through clenched teeth. We hitchhiked back to school in the rain. I never saw Mrs. B. again.

THE STEALING HAD already started. Stella liked to fill vases full of dahlias: amethyst, gold, sapphire, and ruby blooms with emerald leaves, dazzling gems we plucked nightly from the loamy gardens of retirees living near us. Neither of us thought of it as theft.

After Stella's mom died, household items began to appear. Handy things: a vegetable peeler and a potato masher, a small saucepan, a gallon soup pot. An iron, rolls of toilet paper, bath towels. Pretty things: shiny knick-knacks and velvet bed covers. Stella's coat was like Mary Poppins' carpetbag; she'd arrive home, unbutton and disgorge the contents of a kitchenware store or a haberdashery. There were knives and forks and socks and sweaters and dresses and hats and mittens. She'd change out of her fishnets and boots into an elegant dress and high heels, and pin her hair up into a French roll, a disguise to fool unsuspecting storekeepers. Once, she walked into an antiques emporium and picked up a huge nineteenth-century jardinière. She held it out in front like a spinnaker and sailed right out of the store.

WE TALK ABOUT stealing someone's heart, the act of purloining passion that is not ours to take freely. We talk about stealing liberty, to take freedom through unjust means. Maybe this is what compelled Stella to plunder goods without paying. Her mother had been taken, her heart song snatched away. The stealing became her mourning.

AN OLD POEM chimes by Harold Monro, "Overheard on a Saltmarsh." The strange pleading between a goblin and a nymph tells of obsession—the one howls for what he cannot have, the other will not give up what she stole:

> *Nymph, nymph, what are your beads?*
>> *Green glass, goblin. Why do you stare at them?*
> *Give them me.*
>> *No.*
> *Give them me. Give them me.*
>> *No.*
> *Then I will howl all night in the reeds,*
> *Lie in the mud and howl for them.*
>> *Goblin, why do you love them so?*
> *They are better than stars or water,*
> *Better than voices of winds that sing,*
> *Better than any man's fair daughter,*
> *Your green glass beads on a silver ring.*
>> *Hush, I stole them out of the moon.*
> *Give me your beads, I want them.*
>> *No.*

I will howl in the deep lagoon
For your green glass beads, I love them so.
Give them me. Give them.
     No.

Why do we fill our empty spaces with gleaming baubles when it is the entire dazzling moon we desire? We try to grasp light between our fingers, keep love permanent, capture our dear ones in amber. No amount of drinking, cutting, or stealing will suffice.

LEAVING HOME HOLLOWED me out some. My mother's last year's of marriage to my stepfather, then her divorce, made her unavailable to me. I flailed about in my late teen years, trying to figure out life beyond high school routine and my mother's rules. Scrambling about in that first year of college, it felt monumental to just show up on campus. I remember: a professor with a terrible stutter, a class on Grimm's fairytales, an American lecturer who showed slide after slide after slide of Gothic cathedrals, my feet going numb in the winter frost, accompanying Stella to a department store to steal dresses, and a duck egg blue dress with black piping and a wide black belt which I shoved under my coat. Nothing of Stella's burden was obvious to me then. If she wept, it was behind the closed door of her bedroom, muffled by her mandala-patterned bedspread and Indian cotton pillows.

Breaking the law left me feeling dazed, not daring.

Ultimately, I didn't want stuff that much. My good girl programming, a Sunday school thou-shalt-not-steal echo, made me feel uncomfortable and shifty. I did not have a mother-sized void to fill—my mother was alive and may as well have been perched on my shoulder telling me to be good.When I tried to steal a frozen chicken from the corner store, I failed. My bird-numbed arm would not hold. The fowl slid down, thunk, on to the counter. I laid out the bills to pay for it. The storekeeper did not ask why the poultry emerged from my jacket—a magic trick gone wrong. Life was more absurd and sadder than I could manage.

Stella and I never discussed her dead mother or the thieving. No one encouraged us to talk or write about our anguish. What could be said? We stumbled on through our freshman year, until the last semester. Krazy Ken's even crazier girlfriend Faye had a psychotic episode and pulled a knife on us, I don't know why. Stella moved in with friends. I answered an ad to live with four engineering students. My boyfriend cheated with a tall, thin blond law student named Pip. She had a voice that dropped two octaves whenever a man was in her radius. My boyfriend never discussed it with me, he just dropped out of view, stopped visiting, stopped calling. Pip's unexpected pregnancy and subsequent abortion had sucked his energy, he told me years later, when I met him in a French restaurant in another city. His paunch hung over his belt slightly and he worked as a direct mail executive, so the sting seemed very distant. At the time, it was sharp enough to make me transfer to another college and begin again.

I never *intentionally* stole again, although the next year I took a can of tuna from the grocery store around the corner from my student apartment. Woozy from having my wisdom teeth removed a few hours earlier, I walked out with my money in one hand and the can in the other. My mother was present then, her warmth supporting me in the courtroom as I was processed and fined. I was grateful for her there, steadying me.

STELLA WAS THE first of my friends to marry, the first to have children and the first to really become an adult, no longer adrift. She survived breast cancer and outlived her mother in years. One of her daughters visited me recently—between trips to Burning Man and Bali, cycling solo down the Pacific coast from Canada to Baja California—such an intrepid young woman, nothing flaky about her. We laughed at the stories her mother told her—the time I thought I could fly because of a penicillin allergy, the time we left henna in Stella's hair overnight and turned it bonfire orange—and grew quiet recalling the stealing and the unfinished grief.

The freshmen in my classes appear so worldly next to *my* eighteen-year-old self. They visit counselors. They talk to each other. They write about their desolation, their endings. They thaw out their numbness, on the page. We may say we are "at a loss" when we are unsure how to proceed. We may clutch at smuggled trinkets instead of mourning. Sorrow cannot be blotted out by stealing, or by silence. When all we love cannot be reclaimed, words will at least help us remember.

A REGRET

WHEN I WAS twenty, life zigged and zagged, careened and drifted. My adultness was sparse, like new grass growing in. My memory, with time, has also grown patchy. I recall a young girl, wide-eyed and afraid, and brightly dyed silk sarongs, flapping on a clothesline.

That summer, I worked in a summer camp for children. It was a job borne of desperation, not out of interest in children. Dreamy romantics that we were, my friend Anna and I planned a traveling theater show, a caravan of dramatic delights, but by the time our grant money came through the rest of our troupe had already left town for other work. I was broke and needed the money for my third year of college. Tuition was free then in New Zealand, and I had a stipend, but I relied on vacation jobs to pay my bank overdraft. Knocking on doors in the rich part of town, we asked if we could garden. Anna and I weeded for three days, then fled to apple-picking jobs on a faraway orchard. With us came a bolt of Chinese silk, my old knee-operated Elna sewing machine, and a pile of books by Gide, Genet, Rimbaud, and Camus. These authors induced melancholy, angst, and more lying about under the trees than picking fruit. When we did work, we stood atop tall ladders with our heads in apple leaves, in perfect summer heat tempered by salty, decay-scented breezes blowing off a nearby tidal estuary. Beauty, tainted, we thought.

We were fired on the third day.

Our books were not useful for orchard work. Our romance with existentialism was interrupted by anxiety about our empty bank accounts. We had no place to stay and no money. A job in a children's camp was our rescue. Anna and I took our bolt of silk, my old Elna, our books, and hitchhiked three hundred miles to get there.

In our spare time we cut, hemmed, and dyed lengths of silk. They hung glistening on a wire clothesline slung between two posts. Garnet, amethyst, topaz, and lapis sarongs rippled and danced in the summer breeze, gleaming and shimmering in the light stippled through the fruit trees at the camp. Flapping softly, gossamer sighing against gossamer. This is what I recall vividly of that summer.

The rest was not beautiful. This was no happy camp. Marycrest was set on a farm near the sea. It was once a residential school for wayward Catholic girls. The tears and rebellions of those sad teenagers seeped from the dark hallways and dingy linoleum. The laughter and fart jokes of our eight- to twelve-year-old campers did little to diminish the gloom. Our kids had left unhappiness, illness, and brokenness, to give solitary parents respite, to find some small joy with us.

You couldn't call us camp counselors. We had no training, no skills beyond our own childhoods. We could put a band-aid on a grazed knee, or break up an altercation over a toy, or organize a water war, but we didn't think we were *in loco parentis*.

One day, a girl sidled up to me in the hallway, a dim institutional corridor echoing with secret couplings and hidden pregnancies, smelling of damp coats and children's feet. Hannah had curly black hair, skin brown like my own, and wide dark eyes tilting up at me, asking. Asking me to do what, exactly? She mentioned her uncles. The uncles did things to her, repeatedly. Sexual things. She didn't want to go home.

I can conjure up small boys laughing at cowpats. Bus trips to the sea. Ball games, sticky fingers, glue, and the waxy smell of crayons. Silk sarongs dancing on a clothesline. But for the life of me I can't recollect what I said to Hannah, who I told or what I did. I know it was inadequate, whatever I did. Perhaps I told only Anna, but I can't be certain. In the last week of camp, I heard that my stepbrother, of sorts—he was the son of my mother's ex-husband—was killed. He was riding his motorbike, slipped in hot tar, and slid under the back of a truck. He was decapitated. Details did not stick that summer, that year when existentialism caught up with me—without the romance.

I THINK NOW that I was neglectful. Where was my humanity when that little girl confided in me? Does naivety and youthful ignorance mitigate my neglect? These days we are accustomed to seeing politicians, chief executives, bishops, coaches, pastors, sports stars, and institutions getting caught out, covering up, confessing, saying sorry, paying a price, or denying. They litigate. They apologize for transgressing: infidelity, prostitution, insider trading, embezzling, lying. For raping children, for seeing children raped, for knowing children were raped. For muddling things up, messing things up, messing up the muddles, lying about the messes, masquerading. Apologies fly out from them, a story in their defense, a pleading, a sorry song from transgressor to the wronged, to those of us watching. It's as if they make themselves naked for a flogging in the public square. They weep, they call for forgiveness, and we decide to accept. Or not. Maybe I am like them.

There is a village called Regret, near Verdun, France, where eunuchs were enslaved in the fifth century and the French battled the Germans in the World Wars. I would like to take my remorse, or guilt, sin, whatever it is, and leave it beyond the moat, behind the reinforced emplacements at the Fort du Regret. I would like to forget it.

Years later, when I was a mother, I had a second opportunity to help a child. A small boy told me he had been repeatedly molested, coerced, hurt by another child. That time I acted. I was able to listen acutely to what he said and secured his safety. The years had given me maturity and knowledge. I was confident that I could act, that I could prevent further loss for this child.

My mother said, "Two wrongs don't make a right." I've discovered that one right doesn't negate a wrong. My regret, my remorse, still takes up its own space, reminding me that the strong should safeguard the vulnerable, no matter how ineffectual one may feel at the time.

The holiday camp job ended with the season. My friend Anna and I packed up our silk sarongs and sold them at a three-day music festival. The profits would have covered us for the university year, but I carelessly left the money unguarded in our tent. It was stolen, vanished, along with most of my other memories of that summer.

Apart from Hannah with her wide, trusting eyes, and the vision of thirty lengths of silk flapping on a clothesline.

RODENTS

GREY IN THE corner of my eye. From the kitchen sink to the stovetop, streaking along the top of the speckled granite. Swift. Brown-pink feet a blur. Chewed vegetable rind flecks the countertop next to the plastic compost tub. There are bite marks exposing the bright green flesh of two kiwis in the blue glass fruit bowl.

I want to see the dark grey of mouse under the yellow flange of my baited trap, under an ochre dab of peanut butter. I want the silver spring to snap across mouse fur.

Scurrying, nibbling, detestable creatures.

But.

In my childhood books prowled charmers in little smocked dresses and bonnets—adorable. On television danced Disney's rats, Mickey and Minnie—loveable. Once, I sewed my young niece two stuffed toys, a sweet field mouse in a blue spotty dress and a white bonnet, and a rogue French sewer rat with a little moustache, wearing a beret, striped t-shirt, and black stovepipe pants. One—Robbie Burns's "wee, sleekit, cow'rin', tim'rous beastie." The other—a "dirty rat," James Cagney-style. Conflict lies here, between affection and disgust.

In Berlin, I met an entrancing white rat. Before the wall came down, the city of the West was a crazy amalgam of burlesque, Bohemians, punks, and anarchists. People lingered at curbside tables until two in the morning. They slept until ten, meandered to work around eleven, and returned to the streets at dusk when buskers and performers turned the streets into a fairytale. There were stilt walkers, torch song singers, Brazilian dancers, puppeteers, and fish-netted contortionists.

For hours, I watched a couple playing an old wooden barrel organ. She wore black leather, her hair lavender and pink. He wore black lie-on-your-back-to-get-them-on pants. His hair was short and black on one side and shaved around his ear like a lab experiment, with longer blond hair curling like wood shavings on the other side. From his nest of hair popped a small head. A delicate little face, not unlike the man's pointed little chin and narrowed bright eyes. "Annabelle Rat" was immaculate in white fur with pink accessories—smooth tail, long elegant feet under her slender body. She did a little pirouette on the man's shoulders and danced down his arm. I was spellbound. The freedom of these three creatures spoke to me. My holiday was about to end, and I had to fly home to work.

"Come away with us and join our merry band," the dancing creature may have squeaked in her rat language.

"Don't go home to deadlines, your desk with its paper piles, your bills and schedules. Stay a while and twirl."

What small child has not dreamed of running off to join the circus? Here before me was a trio who had created their own street-side ring. How thrilling to be out of the cage, entertaining people and living life emancipated from the nine to five routine, on the edge of the night. It seemed that the characters from my childhood books had come to life.

But.

Rats and mice are dangerous. They harbor the plague, salmonella, monkeypox, and *Streptobacillus moniliformis*, which causes rat-bite fever. On the El in Chicago I was sitting near a man who wafted the smell of antiseptic. He was dressed in Rocawear jeans, sneakers and a patchwork leather jacket with "Pellé" embroidered on the back. But from the jacket sleeve, his oversized forearm and hand stuck out skewed and stiffly bandaged, like Boris Karloff in *The Mummy*.

"I was at work, man, and this thing bit me. I was in the hospital seven days. They give me IV antibiotics three times a day, man. Could have died. They just let me out today," he said.

"You know, rats, they don't have stomachs like we do," he continued. They just have one intestine."

I wanted to tell him it was not true, but a commotion broke out when a crazed man boarded the train. Lurching towards me, he shouted, "I love you, I love you, I want to kiss your feet." I was afraid he might bite them, so I curled my toes up.

A LARGE STAND of Malaysian bamboo bordered our old garden in New Zealand. Thick as drainpipes, the tall stakes harbored rats and mice, a hunting ground for our cats Tutu and Tane. They dragged bloody trophies through the cat door, across the living room carpet, up the stairs. We learned to be cautious about sitting down to breakfast with bare feet.

One Friday night, the patriarch of bamboo rats appeared at the kitchen countertop, just as my husband was unwrapping a bundle of fish and chips. Our young son's eyes were wide as the dinner plates, watching Don Ratticus watching a piece of battered snapper. The rat ran off and hid in a breezeblock holding up my computer workstation, but his dangling tail gave him away.

1. INT. HOME. EARLY EVENING

Theme music to *The Godfather* begins.

HUSBAND

You come into my house uninvited. You come into my house with no respect.

DON RAT

I ask you for justice.

HUSBAND

Now I'm gonna make you an offer you can't refuse. It's time to sleep with the fishes.

Husband traps the rat in the breezeblock, covering each end with a wooden slat and wrapping wire around it. He plans to drown the rat in a bucket of water, with Son as a keen witness.

Enter LA MAMA.

DON RAT

(Pleading)

I apologize if I offended you. I am a stranger in this suburb. And I meant no disrespect to you, or your son.

LA MAMA

It's time to stop this feud. I want no acts of vengeance. Liberate him!

HUSBAND

Someday, and that day may never come, I'll call upon you to do a service for me, like keeping the river rats from my door. But uh, until that day—accept this justice as a gift.

DON RAT

Let me say that I swear on the souls of my grandrats— and there are hundreds—that I will not be the one to break the peace that we have made here today.

EXT. DUSK.

Husband carries breezeblock down into the garden, followed by Son. He sets the block on ground and slowly undoes the wire. Don Rat emerges and flees into the bamboo, without glancing back.

THE NIGHT OF the rat liberation is one I am not allowed to forget. *If* I had grown up on a farm, I would have dispatched the rat, my husband says.

WE LEFT OUR cats behind in our homeland when we moved to Chicago. For years, we lived with no animals, other than the mice that ventured into our apartment every winter. They scrabbled in the walls while I sat at my desk, and scuttled across my feet unless I perched them on the base of my chair. Besieged, I loathed them. Bold marauders, they shimmied like pirates up the toaster cable onto the kitchen table, scattering their telltale droppings like trails of burnt sesame seeds. I found tiny black pellets in my son's bed and up on his bookshelf. It drove me crazy to think of them trekking across his sheets—the uninvited, the unwanted. I set traps.

THAT WAS BEFORE the wanted, the invited, the never trapped. My son requested gerbils, tiny desert rats, as a reward for a good report card.

"Mom, I've done the research. I know what their habitat is. I know what they eat. I'd take care of them."

Then he started on his father: "Dad, I've done the research . . . "

He chose two tiny pets and named them Oreo and Pudding. Shell-colored ears folded in like delicate leather baby shoes. Oreo's big cranberry eyes stared out of birchbark grey fur. She was sized between a mouse and a rat.

Pudding was petite, a soft feather duster sliding through my fingers. For hours, I watched them. Oreo was slower, stronger, and bolder than Pudding. My son nicknamed her Destructor because she shredded empty toilet rolls in minutes. Once she jumped onto her water dispenser, out of the cage and down several feet on to the floor, when the cage lid was left open. I found her trembling in the kitchen the next morning. After, she became obsessive, licking her paws, cleaning her head and ears repeatedly, tidying the cage, flinging bedding around and digging about in the straw. Change unsettled her.

Pudding was fleet of foot, nervy, and squeaked when panicked. She was coquettish and pretty, with silky fur the color of a penny. My son called her Runner Bean, because she dominated the running wheel in her cage. She ran on it for hours. I imagined she imagined she was bounding across the Mongolian steppes, fleeing from the unwanted advances of Genghis Gerbil, running towards Lawrence of the White Robes. She liked to keep her figure trim, and let her sister eat the fatty foods—sunflower seeds.

When the boys watched football, I chilled with "my girls," marveling at their manicured little fingers and shapely pink feet. They smelled like sweet straw when I nuzzled their soft little backs and their frightened hearts beat as fast as a hummingbird's wings if I held them for too long.

I don't know why these little beasties captured me so. My babies were growing up. I lived in a house of males.

My sisters lived far away. Perhaps the rodents became my sisters, my surrogates. *Meriones unguiculatus*, the "clawed warrior" of the proud order of *Rodentia*, under the family crest of *Cricetidae*, had my heart.

One snowy day, we bundled Oreo and Pudding into the car and drove them to a friend for safekeeping while we went to New Zealand. Short-lived safety. I sobbed on the carpeted steps inside Auckland Public Library the day my husband delivered the terrible news. Oreo had bitten Pudding's head off. Two days later, perhaps of remorse, Oreo died. She had never liked change.

AN AUTUMN CHILL overtakes the nights. Mice squirm through the crevices in my home's stone foundations and up through the walls. Occasionally, from my office near the kitchen I hear squeaks. Quietly, I slipper-walk across the hallway. Flash of dark grey. Swift. Into the gap between the stove and cabinets. Gone.

But.

In the dark, at midnight in my bed, I hear the snap of the spring and I wonder at the distinction between the invited and uninvited, the liberated and the caught, the cosseted and the dead.

DREAMTIME

OUR INTERNAL NIGHT music is often fractured by nightmares about our children. The boys, oblivious in their beds, sleep silently while their father and I lurch back and forth from dreams to wakefulness. My husband dreamed that our youngest son fell down a well. He reached in deep to rescue him, and from the musty dark he dragged up a shrunken boy the size of a wet sponge.

WHEN WE TOOK trips in the early years of our parenthood, my sleep was studded with nightmares, the terror of losing or forgetting a child. I dreamed my toddler absconded down Sydney's Oxford Street, as if on mechanical legs. My baby was stolen in Mexico City, his plump ankle slung over his kidnapper's shoulder. I searched for my boys on the rocky outcrops of Arcadia National Park, but their yellow and grey parkas camouflaged them against lichen and cracks. Their starfish bodies drifted in a full moat at the Tower of London. They were hustled away by trench-coated strangers in Times Square, their tiny arms stretched toward me. I never caught them.

Panting, I propelled myself to the surface of waking, listening for my children's breathing. Then I hurtled back into another episode. Averting disaster, I replaced endings and added appendices, replaced what-ifs and if-onlys, until settling upon a soothing narrative to guide me from dark waters and back to contented sleep.

PERHAPS FEARFUL DREAMING provides practice for when we drift on to life's jagged rocks. At the beginning of family life, I felt bathed in the clear light of hope. There was little inkling that the sky could turn green and the wind rotational. A sea change in my slumber let fear seep in as a safeguard against complacency. It was like a homeopathic tincture, immunizing me before any larger ill befell my children.

THE WILDNESS BEGAN when I was first with child. My midnight belly appeared to be a leather sculpture with a relief of contorted primate limbs. "But I don't want a monkey," my dreaming self implored. "I want a real baby."

Weeks later, I unzipped my belly and set my fetus down on the sidewalk to race against a rival. They scampered down the street, translucent creatures, like alien babies. I waited at the finish line, bilious and fevered, grasped my unborn child, and zipped him back inside me to safety. I don't recall who won.

Poring over pregnancy books, I discovered that elevated progesterone levels cause broken REM sleep and increased waking. Pregnant women often dream of non-human progeny. Unzipping bellies are not uncommon.

WE, WHO HAVE had our bodies snatched, need to confront what grows inside the pod. At the library, I checked out *10,000 Dreams Interpreted*, which was written a century ago by Gustavus Miller, a Tennessee merchant and author who claimed that mysterious forces moved his hand across the page. He explained my dreams thus: "If a young woman dreams of a monkey, she should insist on an early marriage, as her lover will suspect unfaithfulness."

I did not have an early marriage, but waited until my child was nine months old.

"Dreaming of anything moving in your belly indicates humiliation and hard labor."

My baby had a posterior position and clutched his hand to his chin. My labor was hard. Humiliation rides alongside childbirth—the gaze of medical strangers upon your swollen genitalia, failing to secure a diaper on a newborn, your laden breasts leaking when you venture to buy milk from the corner store.

"Falling into a well means overwhelming despair will overtake you."

The tiny creature in your house cries for hours—a sharp vibrato then pause, a jagged gasp for breath, followed by another serration, a pause, a gasp, and on. And on. He has come without instructions, and no feeding or diaper changing or singing will stop the crying. Finally, you discover the bump on the floor by a door. If you rock him in his stroller fast back and forth across the bump, the pitch of the howling deepens, the quavering shortens, the gasps lengthen, the noise subsides and he drifts into slumber.

WHILE I WAS dreaming of my fetus, my fetus was dreaming, too. Sonographs detect REM sleep at around twenty-three weeks gestation. In the first three months, "the first thin slivers of memory track begin streaking across the fetal brain," writes Dr. Thomas Verny in *The Secret Life of the Unborn Child*. He says that unborn babies are "processing their own thoughts, feelings and life experiences to date, much as the rest of us do in dreams." What dream within a dream did my water creature have? An *in utero* somersault, the splash and coolness of his mother's swim hours earlier, a languid awareness of morning warmth as the sun slid over the skylight above the bed. I wondered if my panicked imaginings seeped into him. Did he dream in color or in black and white? He writhed and flexed, hiccupped, and stretched in his sleep. When his father arrived home late, he would suddenly become restless, stirring and rolling inside me when footsteps echoed up the side path and the key clattered in the front door lock.

MOTHERS HAVE LONG wondered about the sleepers inside them. Ancient Sumerians wrote about fetal dreams and the inevitable separation of mother and baby, mythologizing them in tales about the great goddess Inanna and her offspring Dumuzi. Cuneiform tablets crafted five thousand years ago tell of heroic battles. In *The Origin of Anxiety*, Franz Renggli writes that they represent the struggles of pregnancy, birth, infancy, and separation. The pictures and stories helped people adapt to a life of alienation, to understand the trauma of birth and the hidden aspects of human dreams before and after birth.

BROKEN SLEEP HELPS train you for insomnia. My first child was born, as planned, with a midwife in our wooden bungalow, so he was home from the beginning—although it took us a week to realize he was there to stay. We woke instinctively to the feeling of being watched, one summer midnight. The red neon sign on the Hydra bacon factory glowed through the French doors, meeting the moonbeams above the bed. Our newborn stared in the silence, his eyes shining in the light. We imagined him communicating psychically to the mothership: "Two of the big ones have got me, but so far, they're treating me well."

EVEN NOW, MY mother finds it hard to fall asleep without thinking of her grown children. When I was a teen, she'd wait up until I arrived home, pacing at the top of the stairs in her floral nightgown, refilling her water glass and checking the time on the grandfather clock. She lies restless in the dark and has nightmares sometimes. "A mother never sleeps well," she says.

WHEN IT LOOKED as though the United States would go to war with Iraq, *L.A. Weekly* reported an increase in women dreaming of Armageddon. In their nightmares, they had to protect their children from soldiers, nuclear bombs, gas, from apocalypse. One pediatrician said all his patients were concerned about the effect of the war on their children. A clinical psychologist, Dr. Lois Nightingale, reported an uptick in post partum depression. She likened it to a collective Jungian dream. "Life-and-death situations intensify the fears of mothers, who instinctually feel threatened by war," she said. "Moms have these fantasies of ways their children could die and they rehearse these possibilities through what-ifs."

MY YOUNGEST SLEPT fitfully, electrified by dreams he could never describe. At two o'clock, I'd hear his feet shuffling on the oak floor or a shift in the air next to me, and I would wake up. He would clamber up and over me, wedging his head under mine, his hair pooling damply on the white sheets. As I sucked up his sweet boy-neck scent, his breathing eased and he would plunge, reassured, into dreamless sleep. So would I, knowing he was safe.

THE DISPLEASURE
OF THE TABLE

MY BOY EATS cantaloupe in the night glow of lamplight. Juice shimmers in his neck hollows and slides down his tawny belly. Teeth sink into soft ripe flesh, sweetness gurgles across lips, splashes onto the oak floor. My boy, like the melon, is luscious and golden, perfect and summery. I want to snort in the scent of his musky hair, drink him in, my own lush fruit, innocent and sweet.

My husband strides in with news that breaks my idyll. A cantaloupe crisis. Listeria. Recall. Hospital admissions. Symptoms appear two to four weeks after eating. Flu-like aches and fever, maybe septicemia, meningitis, spontaneous abortion, even *death*.

If I put my fingers in my ears and hum a happy tune, will the threat go away?

I LOVE TO hear my children slurping and purring at the trough of untidy eating, the decadent joy of politeness abandoned in the privacy of home—sucking up strands of spaghetti, mopping sauce, licking melted ice cream from the bowl. Cooking, eating, and sharing food with my family is a primal act. Transubstantiation—the mother transfers the goodness of leaf and flank to make her children robust. All the joys of fresh food: herby and smelling of dirt and cut grass. Tender salad leaves and cherry toma-toes, plump and melty meat. I set the table for dinner with a cotton cloth and napkins and pink coneflowers from the garden. The candles flicker across the prairie blooms, il-luminating our family of four as we eat and talk. These moments of communion are as fleeting and precious as quicksilver, snatched between soccer and school, work and play. If one of our highest goods is pleasure, let us share it at the table. La dolce vita. Dinner is our magical campfire in the suburbs.

But I worry, I fret. What strange hurts hide in the let-tuce, the strawberries, the chicken, the melon, the spin-ach? What dark poisons may turn the eating violent?

My ears are alert to news of poisoning. A man left his soup out of the refrigerator for twenty-five days. It smelled funny when he put the spoon to his mouth, but he ate it anyway and landed in the hospital for fifty-sev-en days. A toddler sickened after petting a llama. A boy kissed his pet turtle and became ill. These incidents do not faze me—we keep our distance from reptiles, pet-ting zoos, and fermented soups. But when a friend's col-lege-aged, robust football player son lost thirty pounds and almost died after eating a salad, I gasped. *That* could happen to us.

The weekly produce report unhinges me: cantaloupe. Green onions. Sprouts. Ground beef. Hazelnuts. Berries. Cherry tomatoes. Kale. Oysters. Turning pleasure to pain, their accomplices include *e. coli*, botulism, *campy-*

lobacter, hepatitis A, norovirus, *Salmonella*, *Shigella*, necrotizing enterocolitis, *Vibrio*, *Clostridium perfringen*s. The bacteria lurk in supermarket pyramids of shiny fruit and bagged vegetables. There's a recall almost every week, a potential crisis. Cilantro. Eggs. Watermelon. Macadamia nuts. Green beans. Cucumber. Sliced apples. Mushrooms. Cheese. Pine nuts. Tuna. Pickles. Ice cream. Walnuts. Frozen pot pies.

MY MOTHER NURTURED her brood through discipline, gardening, and food. She spent days pruning and digging. I, the youngest of four children at home, spent hours fashioning leaf costumes for fairies and playing in the orange poppies, lulled by the sound of my mother's spade cleaving dirt. At day's end, she cooked dinner and laid a cloth on the dining table. This is how she imposed order, provided unity, and let us know we were safe in our family circle.

Grandmother died when Mother was three. Cooking and gardening and raising children were skills Mother taught herself. She tried out recipes from the Women's Harmonic Society fundraising cookbook: sweet and sour chicken, nasi goreng, curry, risotto, sautéed brains, Hungarian goulash with paprika and green peppers. These dishes seemed exotic compared to the mutton and mashed potatoes that most of our neighbors ate. At the time, salad meant iceberg lettuce ringed with sliced, hard-boiled eggs, and served with jarred mayonnaise, but ours was tossed with lemon vinaigrette in a wooden bowl rubbed with a garlic clove. Mother insisted we try everything. I sat stubbornly for hours one night, refusing to eat ribbons of tripe quivering in a white sauce.

My two older sisters baked, filling the kitchen with the smell of caramelized sugar and vanilla. They made rhubarb crumble, blackberry and apple tart, fluffy lemon meringue pie and—my favorite—chocolate fudge pudding. Whipped cream slid over the warm topping and pooled into an oozy rich sauce in the bottom of the plate. Food was delicious. It was reassurance. It was love.

My mother grew lemons, rhubarb, fruit trees, tomatoes, raspberries, and blackberries behind her fragrant climbing roses, flowering cherries, and azaleas. A pot of spinach sprouted near the back door. The plain Jane of the garden, it padded out meals often short on meat because we lived on my mother's widow's benefit. Spinach was the standby vegetable of my childhood, guaranteed to grow vigorously through mild New Zealand winters. As a child, I wearied of its astringent taste in salads, soups, stews, simmered in butter, but my mother knew it as a reliable source of nutrition.

NOW BAGGED SPINACH joined the danger list, rendered inedible by *e. coli* 0157:H7, a tidy little rod-shaped bacteria that is particularly toxic to humans. Commercial beds of spinach were sprayed with watered-down cow feces carrying the lethal pathogen. Across twenty-six states, two hundred people got sick, vomiting and purging streams of bloody diarrhea. The bacteria killed a two-year-old and an elderly woman. They contracted hemolytic uremic syndrome, where the red blood cells die off and the central nervous system breaks down, causing hallucinations and tremors. Damage done to the occipital cortex causes blindness. The kidneys fail, then the heart.

Spinach has me rocking, teetering, cracking. I dreamt about it, in a Salvador Dali meets Julia Child meets William Wordsworth montage, a nightmarish mash-up. I wandered into a host of—not golden daffodils—green spinach. The cluster waved to me from a hillside, then melted like Dali's clocks, screaming into a steaming pot in Julia Child's tiny French kitchen. I woke sweating. Spinach has become biohazard, not rescue.

Our modern habits—eating outside our homes, savoring summer treats in winter, expecting cheap, globally sourced food—exact a high price. Contamination creeps in at every step: growth, manufacture, distribution, preparation, and consumption. Each year, around forty-eight million Americans get sick from foodborne diseases. Three thousand die.

AMERICA IS ON alert for terrorists. The towel guy in my gym asked me when I came back from a visit to family in London: "Weren't you afraid of terrorists?"

"No," I replied. "Who needs terrorists when we have the American food chain? I'm more likely to be killed by eating *spinach*."

I want that powerhouse of iron, its potassium and thiamin, its A and C, its carotenoids and folic acid. Spinach was never the glamour vegetable at the greengrocers, like truffles, champignons or mâché. Never a star, except in a can for Popeye. Flemish still life paintings highlight sculptural artichokes or cabbages. Arcimboldo's portraits feature endives, fennel root, celeriac, and parsnips. Not spinach. It's not on screen in *Babette's Feast* or *The Cook, The Thief, His Wife & Her Lover*. There's no novel called *Spinach*, lining the shelves next to *Fried Green Tomatoes*, *Peeling the Onion* or *The Princess and the Pea*.

Spinach originated in Southwest Asia. The name derives from a Persian word ispanai, or "green hand." In China, it was the "herb of Persia," and in England, the "Spanish vegetable," after the Moors introduced it to Europe via Spain. Italian Catherine de Medici gave us a la Florentine—"on a bed of spinach." The vegetable doesn't have a place in history like corn and squash, forever celebrated in national mythmaking at Thanksgiving. Even the potato—once considered the evil cause of poor work attitude, birth defects and flatulence—has ten museums around the globe. The blight, *Phytophthora infestans*, destroyed the spud in 1840s Ireland, contributed to the Great Hunger, and led to the diaspora of starving refugees across the globe. Irish corn was shipped off to England, while the Irish people's food "melted in rottenness on the face of the earth," according to Irish nationalist John Mitchel. "The Almighty indeed sent the blight, but the English created the Famine." My Irish forbears, Waltons and Nealies, ended up in New Zealand. I understood early that people could be murdered with food, just as they could be nourished. We create powerful legends around sustenance.

On wet Sunday afternoons when I was a kid, I watched re-runs of old cartoons, including one featuring an unlikely hero, *Popeye the Sailor.* "I'm strong to the fin-ich / 'Cause I eats me spin-ach," sang E.C. Segar's cartoon character. He tripled the American public's consumption of the canned vegetable in the 1930s. The humble green is a rock star in the rural states. Ours is a nation of memorials, including monuments to spinach.

Chester, Illinois, is the proud "Home of Popeye." The muscular sailor tops the banner of the town's website. Sitting on a bluff overlooking the Mississippi, in Mark Twain country, the town of 2,600 people and eleven churches boasts a six-foot Popeye statue with bloated bronze cheeks and oversized forearms, five other statues from the cartoon strip, and a three-day celebratory annual picnic.

The city of Alma, Arkansas, the self-proclaimed Spinach Capital of the World, hosts an annual festival with an all-you-can-eat contest of canned spinach. Two water towers are painted green to resemble the largest spinach cans anywhere. Popeye is celebrated with two statues, including one commissioned *after* the major *e. coli* scare. Thieves repeatedly stole one statue, until the city chained it in place.

Crystal City in Texas, another claimant to Spinach Capital of the World, crowns Miss Spinach at its festival each year. In 1937, *Design Magazine* said of the city's Popeye, "The erection of this statue in the heart of the world's greatest spinach-growing country will be a fitting tribute to the man who has made both young and old alike 'Spinach-conscious.'"

Lenexa, Kansas, offers guests at its festival the opportunity to sample the world's largest spinach salad, enter a spinach recipe contest, or put their babies in the Swee' Pea baby crawling contest.

On goes the list.

When I was a kid, Mother enticed me to eat spinach by singing the Popeye song. My children eat the chopped leaves cooked in pies and blended into bolognaise, but never fresh or alone on a plate. While I am afraid of possible pathogens, the boys are suspicious of undisguised vegetables in plain sight. I read them Dr. Seuss's tale about getting frightened by spooky pale green pants with nobody inside them:

> *Then one dark night in Grin-itch*
> *I had to do an errand there and*
> *Fetch some Grin-itch spinach . . .*
> *. . . I lost my Grin-itch spinach*
> *But I didn't even care*

I *do* care about losing my spinach. I want my eggs Florentine back, golden yolk oozing over emerald, just how it should be on the color wheel. I want my spanikopita, the first crunch of crisp buttery pastry sticking to my teeth followed by a creamy blend of feta and spinach. I want my baby spinach leaves mixed into a salad of mesclun, herbs and lettuce, balancing a palette of pale, mid and deep green, maybe walnuts sprinkled over and a few daubs of chèvre.

POPEYE MAY HAVE eaten his spinach canned, but it's best eaten freshly cooked or raw. George Orwell claimed in 1937, "We may find in the long run that tinned food is a deadlier weapon than the machine gun." Processing can harbor botulism, and the plastic introduced in the 1960s to protect us from contaminants contains its own risk—the possibly carcinogenic chemical bisphenol-A.

Fresh spinach is rich in vitamins K, A, C and B, as well as the minerals manganese, folate, magnesium and iron. It contains lutein, an antioxidant which protects our eyes from macular degeneration, anti-cancer compounds, and heart-protecting enzymes. You can understand why parents blend it into baby food and whip it into smoothies for their kids, with no thought to the killer lurking in the food processor.

FOOD AS CURE is a concept central to my family lore. My great-aunt Valmai was a health nut who avoided coffee, alcohol and meat. My Indian grandfather Wally was a "doctor" who claimed to cure people through his natural herbal remedies. This was not a perspective shared with the judiciary, which claimed he killed patients. Opium is a natural derivative of plants and was a popular ingredient of tonics in the early last century. It was also used in ayurvedic healing and the sattvic diet of seasonal food practiced by ancient Indians, several millennia before the Greek physician Hippocrates said, "Let food be thy medicine and medicine be thy food." In 1826, Frenchman Anthelme Brillat-Savarin wrote, "Dis-moi ce que tu manges, je te dirai ce que tu es," a sentiment that 1960s nutritionist Victor Lindlahr converted to, "You are what you eat."

This web of health food philosophies binds Auntie Val, of Irish-Cornish-Wiltshire heritage, her Punjabi brother-in-law—my grandfather—and me. My sister worked in a health food store and got me a weekend job after college. The shop smelled of ground cumin and patchouli. People brought in their own containers and I drizzled local honey into jars, shoveled beans sprouts into plastic pots and henna into cellophane bags. We sold arnica, calendula cream and homeopathic potions, and my sister sold her own homemade tofu makers. This was years before organic produce was readily available in supermarkets.

The modern whole foods trend dates back to the famous Seventh Day Adventist Dr. John Harvey Kellog, who operated the Battle Creek Sanitarium in Michigan in the late 1800s. In order to promote good digestion, he advocated a vegetarian diet, yogurt enemas, exercise, and abstinence from alcohol and tobacco. Eradicating masturbation was another of his obsessions. He didn't make much headway with the latter, but peanut butter and corn flakes were hugely successful.

One of Kellog's acolytes, Edward Halsey, set off in 1900 for far-flung New Zealand, coincidentally around the same time that my herbalist grandfather arrived from India. Halsey began Sanitarium, today a thriving Australasian health food company famous for Wheat-Bix breakfast cereal and Marmite yeast spread. The company also ran vegetarian cafes until the 1960s, way ahead of kale fervor.

Auntie Val was the only Seventh Day Adventist in a family of Methodists. She lived alone with her pet goat Billy, and didn't smoke cigarettes or partake of any other vices outlined in Dr. Kellog's tracts. (I don't know her stance on masturbation, but she was single her entire life.) "I can't eat that," she told Mother. "It wouldn't be good for my digestion. No, I don't eat that either."

She blasted around town on a tricycle powered by a two-stroke lawn mower engine, eating at Hare Krishna cafes in their 1970s heyday. She was healthy and spry until her death at ninety-seven. In a photograph, she climbs through her front window, a leg flung over the sill, her white hair haloed by billowing lace curtains. She was the only relative I knew, aside from my mother and siblings, and she formed part of our family's own mythology of food. She influenced my mother's vegetable-oriented cuisine, a catalyst for the pot of spinach by the door.

MY MOTHER STILL grows a bunch at her back door, in a pot with sorrel and arugula. She picks a few leaves to add to her salad or steam for dinner. Hers is a victory garden of sorts, evading the enemy toxins in industrialized food. She drinks a glass of sherry before setting her table for one, a placemat, a napkin, a rose in a bud vase, her home-cooked meal.

Thousands of miles from my mother, I set my table. Anxiety has seeped into our everyday life—guns in our schools and movie theaters, wars on our television screens, violence in our domestic sphere. It torpedoes la dolce vita. Our food has not come from the garden to the table, the local farm to the plate, in the way it did when I was young. Pathogens in the spinach or cantaloupe could pull the cloth from my pretty table. I fear that neither candles nor flowers will keep my children from sickness. My mother mended and strengthened her children with the five food groups. I wonder, will I *kill* mine?

BEQUEATHED

IVORY:

I pranced about my childhood garden under the honey-suckle hedge, wearing a long rope of ivory beads, flapper-style. Hanging down past my knees, the necklace was a gift from my grandfather Wally to my grandmother Gladys. It was passed on to my mother, who was three years old when her mother died.

My grandparent's marriage was a great romance, in my imagination. I envisaged my grandmother as a young woman, her bone-china skin flushing pink at the throat, her long auburn hair blowing in a soft wind. My grandfather, an Indian prince, darkly handsome, declared his devotion and swept her away on an elephant decked out in velvet and gold. They swayed through date palms and turbaned fan bearers in a distant land, a geography muddled in my mind. The ivory beads were a token of the prince's passion. I marched in the love pageant behind the elephant, jeweled beasts and veiled dancers. It was a grand procession, part circus, part *One Thousand and One Nights*, part *Gone with the Wind*—a child's fantasy, woven under the honeysuckle.

Singing loudly, clambering through the paspalum grass, I wielded a large pair of hedge clippers, heavy in my small hands. I was prepared to knight the groom, chop down a giant, or slay a dragon in my tale. The clippers sliced through the strand, sending the beads tumbling and spilling through the undergrowth.

I kept the loss to myself. My mother asked me if I had seen her precious keepsake. "I saw it in your pigskin purse," I lied. I never told my mother what happened to the broken heirloom.

MEDALS:

My grandfather was an herbalist. When I was a child, the idea of curing people with herbs was exotic and fascinating. I loved opening Mother's miniature carved Indian chest with its spicy waft of camphor and sandalwood. In it nested a collection of medals commemorating his patients' cures. Wrapping my small fingers around the cool circles of bronze and gold, I would sniff their metallic tang, roll their smooth edges along my nails and press them to my cheek. Each engraved with a name, date and the words "Cured by M. Salaman," they noted the peculiar disorders that he had eased. They were frightful things such as "innards trouble," "mental trouble," "tubercular on the sacrum." I memorized the mysterious inscriptions without understanding the ailments or the cures, then slipped the medals back into their sanctuary and secured the brass clasp. I knew to never ask my mother if I could take this treasure to school for show and tell.

My grandfather's mausoleum was a place of mystery. Mosque-like, it stood huge and silent on a flat green clearing in the old part of the New Plymouth cemetery, in the North Island of New Zealand. The minarets and arches made me think of an exotic world of carpets and spices. It sat enveloped in the old lady scent of hydrangeas and aphids, and the musty, damp earth odor dripping from green ferns.

When I was ten we moved back to my birthplace, after years in other places. My mother and I often took long walks through the shaded river reserve on the edge of the suburbs, under ancient tree ferns the size of Jurassic palms, past the graves, to the sea. In hushed tones, my mother told my siblings and me not to tell anyone it was our grandfather in there. I accepted the tomb's looming presence amongst the Protestants, under their greening stone angels and tilting crosses, but I didn't think about who was inside and I didn't ask questions.

I knew the Himalayas were present in my mother's family tree. They were obscured by memories of Cornwall on my grandmother's side—the Methodists and Anglicans and Press Button Bs, as we called Presbyterians. Great-Grandma Richards, with her tight bun and sensible shoes, apparently wasn't overjoyed in the 1920s when her daughter Gladys, with her alabaster skin and thigh-length chestnut hair, married a brown-skinned interloper.

Most of what I know of my grandfather Abraham

Walley Mohammad Salaman, known as Walli or Wally, comes from what I read as an adult, living in America. He was born in Amritsar, in the Punjab region of India in approximately 1885. Apparently, he sailed from India as a teenager and arrived in New Zealand around 1903, but no one knows for sure. A silk merchant, he married Marjorie Cardno, a young Scottish-born woman. They had a child, then split up. Their divorce and nasty custody battle was in the newspapers, their daughter reported as "half-caste."

Wally set up his herbalist business and married my grandmother Gladys Richards in 1924. From a land on the other side of the empire, Wally was Muslim and dark-skinned. British colonists aimed to recreate a "Britain of the South," with ideas of racial purity. Interracial marriage was legal, but not socially desirable. Wally and Gladys had Valerie, my mother, in 1928. She took after her father, with black hair and olive skin. I, too, inherited his olive skin, his dark hair.

PHOTOGRAPHS:

Rita was the receptionist in the newspaper office where I worked nights during my young adult what-am-I-doing-with-my-life-phase, between university and journalism school. My job was looking after the teleprinters that chugged out news from around the world, in the era before newspapers went digital. I liked to escape the smoky newsroom and the sputum-clogged coughs of the old newspapermen and head downstairs to see Rita. She was in her seventies, but still blond, and she kept her hair wrapped in an up-do. She liked to talk. We discovered that we were from the same hometown. Her older sister had worked as my grandfather's secretary until his death in 1941. Rita's sister had long since died, but Rita inherited an envelope of photographs from her. She gave them to me.

Previously, I'd only seen a single image of my grandfather Wally, a man wearing a white cravat gazing directly into the camera. Framed in a dark brown folding card, the yellowing relic was kept with a stack of ancient photographs of my maternal family in a plastic bag on the top shelf of my mother's writing desk.

Rita presented me with six photographs of a dead man and a funeral. I had never seen a dead person or been to a funeral. I hadn't thought about my grandfather during my adolescence or university years, or really even thought about him as a real person. The man I saw now was not a young prince from a fairytale, but a real human, albeit a dead one. I'd had no relationship with this man. My friends had living grandfathers who played lawn bowls and went fishing. Mine died long before I was born.

The first photograph shows a procession of cars, dark Lincolns with running boards and curvaceous bodies, and hundreds of suited men walking, hats in hands, up the cemetery road to a distant chapel. Two of the photographs are of the mausoleum. The tomb is whiter than

I remember from my childhood walks. It is the size of a small house, but so tall that the black-suited attendant reaches only halfway up the doors, the top of the dome the height of another three people standing on his head. The big double doors are open. The cemetery is young and uncluttered, with fledgling trees and empty cow paddocks beyond. Little girls cluster together in pale cotton dresses and the boys wear school shorts and knee-high socks. Women gather on a hill, heads dipped to neighbor, shoulder to shoulder. People stand before and behind the tomb, some astride graves, several perched on top of headstones. There are thousands of people.

A dark coffin of highly polished oak panel features in two photographs. It has six hefty handles and brass floral friezes fixed to the top and sides. Oversized urns of blowsy hydrangeas and smaller vases of daisies flank the coffin, which sits on a terrazzo floor, up against wood-paneled walls inside the tomb.

There is my grandfather, laid out on a bed-sized platform with ornately embroidered pillows and coverlet. He is small, his bare face like a walnut. Shrouded in silk, his arms are tucked tightly to his sides. The silk is green, embroidered with silver, I read later in a library record. My grandfather doesn't look particularly dead. He looks like someone trying to lie very still, keeping very quiet.

I took the photographs and hurried back upstairs to the newsroom to tear the day's news from the teleprinters. I kick myself now for not asking Rita questions. What he was like? What was his wife like? Did she remember his daughter? I put the photographs in a manila envelope and secured the brass fastener. I carried it around with me, through four relationships, to nineteen houses, to five cities in four countries. A lot of distance was needed before I could really look and see the images.

WHISPERS:

Grave robbers stole the monumental bronze doors from my grandfather Wally's mausoleum, sheared them from the hinges, with the thick chain and hefty padlock still entwined. They sliced the dulled brass crescent moon and star from on top of the tomb's blue dome and daubed graffiti across the white stone walls.

My mother was horrified when the council called to tell her; the locks were blown apart—along with my mother's cover. The identity of the man in the tomb was known. At the time, I suspected my mother's horror was not merely at the defilement, but fear of the council demanding money for cleanup costs.

"I think I'll just lie low and hopefully they'll forget about me," she told me on the telephone, a little catch in her honeyed tone. She wanted the council to overlook her.

Years later, I realized she was ashamed of being linked to the carving on the lintel: Mohammed Islam Salaman Tomb. She didn't want people to remember she was Wally Salaman's daughter.

TOLERANCE:

My grandfather was an affluent businessman in the last part of his life, a merchant and the owner of substantial landholdings. He bought ten plots in the New Plymouth cemetery and built a tomb in preparation for death. His was the first Muslim funeral in New Zealand. A Presbyterian minister officiated. It was 1941, the Japanese had just ambushed Singapore, the so-called "Asian menace" was submarining into Australasian waters. Some of the crowd at the funeral would have had boys in service, dying on surf-washed coral outcrops in the Pacific.

Reverend J.C. Wilson, in his white dog collar, stumbled through an Arabic sura of the Qur'an and buried my grandfather.

"It may seem strange to some of you—a Christian minister conducting the funeral of a Mohammedan," he said.

"No clergyman of his faith is in New Zealand, and we should like to think that were we to die in some land of Islam, similarly situated, there might be found some Sheikh of their religion who would give us a Christian burial."

FAIRYTALES:

The mayor of my hometown received an odd letter from Lahore, Pakistan, from a Colonel (Retired) Rafi Nasim. As Col. Nasim sorted through his late father's files, he discovered letters between siblings—his father and my grandfather. Rafi Nasim was a distant cousin, part of an extended family unknown to me.

"Having lost touch with [Wally] sixty years ago has spurred a burning desire to trace his children or grandchildren," Rafi wrote.

He entreated the mayor to find the address of any relatives.

"By doing such a noble thing, you will be doing great service to our family. Please remember Lord Mayor, we will remain in a state of suspense till we receive a reply from you."

Rafi, my mother's cousin, had a view of my grandfather that was as romantic as the one I held when I was small.

"As a child I heard lots of fairytales about my mother's uncle Wally Mohammad having sailed in a ship to unknown places and ultimately landing in New Zealand. It sounded as adventurous as the voyage of Sinbad the sailor. There was no other young man in the family as bold, with the will power, adventurous spirit and the indomitable courage. To leave home as a teenager in search of knowledge or adventure, travel around the world, achieve a respectable position in an alien society and emerge as a successful business man and world renowned herbalist, [he] must be a man of steel."

EPITAPH:

Before I moved to Chicago, a documentary maker called me at home. He was producing a television show about famous graves. I don't recall how he knew that I was related to Wally Salaman, and had photographs, which he asked to borrow. They appeared in a program called *Epitaph* that asserted my grandfather was a rogue, a charlatan, that he had killed people with his herbal remedies, that he had gone to prison. I didn't know any of this or if it was true, but he was charged with the death of a child. A book accompanied the television show. I don't recall seeing either. My mother was upset. I was too, on her behalf, but I had two young children and a job preoccupying me. I thought of the medals that I used to hold and kept the disconcerting knowledge of my grandfather's conviction at a distance.

A TRUST:

My grandfather left a large parcel of farmland in trust for my mother and her children. She sold the land after I was born and it was converted into a subdivision. The trust no longer exists. My mother used all the money to raise six children after my father died when I was seven years old. What remains is the Salaman Reserve, in my hometown. On a map, the green park snakes between grey tracts of houses. When the town celebrated its 150th year of post-colonial settlement in 1991, my mother and my sister planted a kahikatea tree, a native pine, on behalf of my family. I imagine it is tall and straight by now.

DENIALS:

Gita and I smile out of our school field hockey photograph. Wearing checked gingham gym slips and long socks, rows of girls hold hockey sticks before them. In their midst, we are the two dark-eyed, dark-skinned girls with dark shiny pigtails and smiles more dazzling white than those around us. When I turned thirteen, I cut off my pigtails for a Ziggy Stardust mullet and remade myself listening to David Bowie and Lou Reed. I cut off my friend, too. Her parents were Indian and owned a fruit market.

My mother went for a drive with a friend a few years ago, who pointed out a new subdivision and said disparagingly, "That's where the Pakis live." My mother said to me on the phone later, "I hope she doesn't think we are Pakistani."

A hierarchy existed, a good immigrant/bad immigrant bifurcation. Pakistanis—Muslims like my mother's father—were clearly on the wrong side of the suburban divide.

ARTIFACTS:

When great-aunt Valmai passed away in her ninety-seventh year, her executors shipped to my sister a camphor chest full of family memories and all that remains of our grandmother Gladys. It contained a stack of gilt-framed oils of New Zealand landscapes painted by my great-grandfather. One—a sharp peak in a still fjord—now hangs in my Chicago living room. Tiny photographs of the Richards family show my great-uncle Keith in uniform waving as he set off to fight in Gallipoli. The young sisters Gladys and Valmai are dressed in flapper dresses, revealing scandalous stockings.

I opened an envelope full of my grandmother Gladys' soft coppery hair, its smell conjuring up images of youth and dancing and hopefulness, before she met my grandfather Wally Salaman, before he went to prison, before they fled to India, before she was cast aside, before her bone china skin took on the translucent pallor of tuberculosis.

LOSS:

On my last visit home to New Zealand, my mother showed me a letter from her mother. The ink was so faint on the fine yellowing paper that I had to squint to read it. Gladys, my grandmother, wrote to her family from the sanatorium where she was being treated for tuberculosis. How she missed her baby daughter, she wrote. The nurse was pleased with her progress and she hoped to be well enough to see them soon. She sent money to buy my mother a silver bangle.

With the letter was a studio photograph, featuring a wide-eyed, tawny toddler sitting naked on a rug, the silver bangle around her plump wrist.

My mother's mother never came home.

"I miss my mother terribly, I long for her. It's as if there's a hole in my life," my mother tells me often.

KEEPSAKES:

When a woman is ashamed of her heritage, she tries to stay silent about what she inherited. As a child, my mother was ashamed that her father ate pungent foods, that she was dark-skinned among white children, that a chauffeur drove her to school while her classmates walked, that a model of the Taj Mahal sat on the living room mantel. She doesn't tell her children about her father going to prison. She doesn't talk about his family. A chilly river of shame, fear and un-belonging ran through her early years and spilled into adulthood.

I am her youngest child. From the distance of America, I can poke away at all that I've inherited, these keepsakes of loss, racism, shame, tolerance and love. My childish fantasies about heritage dissolved with time and knowledge, lost with the ivory beads. Now I decide what to hold on to, what to let go of, and what to pass on.

THE
MILES
BETWEEN
ME

THE SEDIMENT OF FEAR

I WAS AFRAID. The man behind the glass partition leafed through my papers and asked me something in a language I didn't understand. "I speak only English," I replied. Avoiding my gaze, the man flicked his eyes from the papers to me to the papers. His grey sports jacket shone slightly at the elbows, a middle button dangling from loosened threads. His maroon shirt was undone at the top, no tie. The room echoed, its rows of grey plastic chairs empty. This was a space intended for many, but I was the only person on this side of the barrier. I had stepped into a geography both foreign and startling.

In a corner, green prayer mats lay rolled on a filing cabinet. Separating the main room from a large alcove was a rosewood screen embedded with golden tendrils. Beyond the screen I saw a Pakistani flag and the Stars and Stripes flanking a green table, over which hung wrinkled portraits of Pakistan's founder Muhammad Ali Jinnah, the eleventh president Asif Ali Zardari, and the seventeenth prime minister Raja Pervaiz Ashraf. The walls of the broad space were decorated with photographs of remote desert valleys, mountain peaks, and ancient forts. My planned journey seemed tangible, no longer imagined, and I felt uneasy.

MOMENTS EARLIER, I was being jostled along the Magnificent Mile with clusters of pre-holiday shoppers, past storefront windows full of Italian lingerie, hockey memorabilia, Disney toys, and bright candy. Tourists in puffy jackets were clustered around a plaque set against the polished granite base of the building I needed to enter. A Chicago landmark. "This outstanding Art Deco-style skyscraper helps define one of the city's finest urban spaces," read the inscription. "Its prominence is further heightened by the jog in Michigan Avenue, where it crosses the Chicago River." Peering up to where the guide pointed, I saw Native Americans, traders, soldiers, settlers, and oxen trudging in bas-relief across the limestone wall five floors up. I imagined the riverbank of yesteryear: the crop-tending, fur-hunting, and domestic routines, and the ambushes, massacres, and rifts between competing peoples. This commemorative sculpture, on the site of old Fort Dearborn, demands that we pay attention to the past. It reminds us of conquest, of what is gained and lost.

I stepped from the rowdy street into a silent, gleaming foyer. Roaring Twenties extravagance: verde antico, marble wainscots, and mahogany trim. A sleek monument to the glitter of its time, it was built only fifty years after the Great Fire of Chicago burned down what remained of Fort Dearborn. Hewn from deposits in Minnesota, Indiana, and Greece, the stone is the type used for cathedrals, cenotaphs, tombstones, and the countertops found in seventy-five percent of America's new kitchens. Quarried and transported across borders, these are the rocks that become a surface for our history.

An elevator with bronze birds sculptured on the doors shuddered up to the eighth floor, opening into a corridor with linoleum floor and several sets of identical opaque glass doors. At a dim end, I pressed a buzzer and one door opened.

THE MAN BEHIND the glass examined my pile of documents: application, invitation, passport, green card, employment letter, sponsor's identification. A staccato of questions fired through an aperture:

Who is your sponsor?

My mother's cousin.

Why are you going?

To attend my mother's cousin's granddaughter's wedding. To meet family in Pakistan. To visit the homeland of my mother's father, Amritsar, across the border in India.

One moment. The man walked out of my vision. I heard a door open and click shut. I was alone in the lofty room, with the rows of empty chairs.

I stood there with my disquiet. My feet sounded tinny on the tiled floor. I tried to slow my breathing, to stop its shallow rasp and soften the sharpness in my chest. My anxiety rested on getting a visa, two visas, before I could travel to Lahore in Pakistan, then Amritsar in India, the next month. This type of paranoia bubbled up when I faced bureaucracies with changeable and inexplicable rules. I dreaded the sentries overseeing the secondary interview rooms where one could be isolated or made invisible. Recalling a train ride I took years ago, from a former Eastern bloc country to northern Italy, I saw a faint blue drift of cigarette smoke inside; a blur of damp spring fields outside. The travelers are in good spirits, a mixture of ladies wearing floral headscarves, backpackers, young men laughing in the seats behind me. The carriage quiets as several drab-uniformed soldiers, guns slung across their bodies, sway down the aisle checking documents. One stops at my seat, flips the pages of my passport and barks: "Your visa expires tomorrow!"

"I leave today," I reply. The train slows in a muddy landscape and stops at a white checkpoint station. I can't decipher its sign, written in Cyrillic. The soldiers disembark, taking with them a group of young men, including those who had sat behind me. They don't return.

MY PALMS DAMPENED. As much as I longed to go to Pakistan, I jittered. Bombs and kidnappings dominated the news, although my relative Rafi assured me that his city was safe. My mother worried that my emails were scrutinized. Is the C.I.A. keeping tabs on visitors? Would traveling there impede my re-entry to the U.S.?

I was, I am, a coward. My world is small these days, a domestic sphere of children and husband and dog, neighbors who chat while I tend the garden, friends and colleagues who share interests in writing or teaching. The unfamiliar, the unknown rises up, an oppression that threatens to swamp me.

I felt uneasy about meeting a family of strangers, of answering questions and trying to shore up the rift between generations and continents. I picked my fingernails and turned to look at the photographs of immense mountains and deep gorges of rocks. I saw ravines of grey, brown, and black. Shale, limestone, schist, graywacke, feldspar, soapstone, marble, dolomite, sandstone, granite, born from the earth's thrusting and flowing. Rock created from eruptions, fault lines, folds and cleavages, conglomeration and sedimentation, displacement, and ruptures.

Years ago, my husband and sons began giving me rocks: heart-shaped stones, black and white pebbles washed up on Atlantic beaches, gems tumbled smooth, a carved greenstone from New Zealand, speckled souvenirs from the Great Lakes.

When we excavate the earth, what do we bring from the past into our future? How do the sediments connect us to our earlier selves, our heritage, our conflicts and rifts, our disrupted families?

A DOOR CLICKED open. The man returned to his post behind the glass. He cleared his throat. I stepped over to the aperture. He looked closely at the Invitation For Marriage, which described the celebration ahead:

1. the Nikah ceremony (marriage agreement), to be

performed by a religious celebrant including exchange of rings,

2. the Mehndi, for the bride, where henna is applied
   on the bride's hand; to be followed by a night
   of music,

3. the Mehndi for the groom,

4. the Marriage ceremony,

5. the Walima, a celebration of the marriage.

The letter said: "You will live in our home as a family
guest. It will be a matter of pleasure for us to arrange your
reception, entertainment, and sightseeing."

MY SISTER AND I shopped for these five events—she
in London and I in Chicago—for different outfits, bright
silky pants, tunics, and gauzy scarves embroidered with
sequins and faux gems. Costumes, unlike our usual jeans
and boots, so we could play the part of wedding guests
without appearing alien.

I explained to the man that my mother's cousin extended the invitation when he visited his siblings in Toronto, where they had migrated many years ago. I flew
to meet him for the first time just months earlier. Now, I
planned to meet my sister in Lahore. She would travel
from her home in London. Together, we would represent
multiple generations of our New Zealand family. After the
wedding, my sister would fly home, while I would cross
the border with my relative's friends, stay in their Chan-

digarh house, then travel on alone to my grandfather's ancestral hometown, Amritsar.

This seemed a lot to tell a stranger.

MY GRANDFATHER ABRAHAM Wally Mohammad Salaman, a British subject in colonial India, sailed across the oceans to the Dominion of New Zealand. In the early 1900s, he married my grandmother, whose forbears had migrated from Cornwall. My grandfather died in 1945, before India's independence and the bloody separation of India and Pakistan, two years shy of a 1947 law change that would have granted him New Zealand citizenship. My grandfather was British when he died. I knew him only from photographs, an unsmiling, clean-shaven man wearing a waistcoat with a fob watch on a chain, and pince-nez spectacles in the style of Theodore Roosevelt. My mother—and then my siblings and I—were stranded from extended family in the way of so many separations, without the bedrock of history to either anchor us or stand in our way. Part of my worry was embedded in familial angst. The fossils of racism and worry about heritage—passed from my forebears and inherited by my mother—had washed up on my banks. I wanted to bring our family's ossified connection to life, to stake a claim to that part of my heritage.

Is it possible to have a multiple-entry visa?
No, it is not possible.

I wish to travel to Amritsar from Lahore.

It is not possible.

But I really want to go to Amritsar.

No, it is not possible. You must leave Pakistan and you will not be allowed back.

But I am flying in and out of Lahore.

It is not possible to provide you a multiple-entry visa. You are applying from a third country. He pushed my green cardboard folder back under the window, making it clear that persistence would result in no visa at all. I pushed it back.

Can I have a single-entry visa?

Yes, that is possible. Come back on Monday afternoon at three o'clock.

Outside, I barely recognized Wacker Drive. The river glinted graphite as it coursed toward Lake Michigan. Disappointment scalded my cheeks. I felt inconsequential.

MY QUEST FOR an Indian visa was outsourced to a global corporate enterprise, starting on my home computer and finishing at a booth in a city business center. Impersonal compared to the Pakistani consulate approach, the pursuit began with an online form. Boxes ticked: a six-page printed checklist including the visa application form, a digital visa photograph, a copy of the online order form, two signatures, my passport, my two-inch-by-two-inch photograph glued, not stapled, a photocopied proof of address, my permanent resident card. Documents paper-clipped, not stapled, in order.

I rode the El to Adams and Wabash, walked a block to State Street, and through a door between a sandwich franchise and a cosmetics chain. Inside, a room the size of two tennis courts was sectioned by rope. A slow snake of people moved through the labyrinth to a row of "consultants" sitting in booths behind a long glass window. Behind them, more clerks stapled documents and checked computer records. Processing visa applications to India seemed quite an industry, like a scene from Richard Scarry's kid's book *Busy Town*. I was one in a bustle of overheated bodies peeling off overcoats, shuffling papers, nattering about forthcoming journeys to see grandparents, a yoga retreat, favorite places in a guidebook. A stranger told me about a tea plantation tour somewhere, Darjeeling? A skipping, singing child knocked over a rope barrier. In this room of bright chatter and warm lights, I felt my fear dislodging.

The consultants accepted documents under the glass and talked loudly through slatted portholes at the applicants. A young man slowly counted a pile of bank notes and slid them across the counter, but was short a few dollars and rushed off to the bank. A woman with blonde hair piled up on her head scrabbled in a very *large* velvet bag. Perhaps if she paid attention to the *small* purse instruction on the checklist, she may have discovered her missing photographs. Her visa could not be processed. She cajoled and simpered, shouted, then left in a flurry of perfume. My turn. Gleaming the kind of smile you see in tourist brochures, a woman clerk glanced quickly at my documents. She asked me no questions about my purpose or whom I would visit. She gave no indication that she recognized me as a descendant of India or even cared. But she would ensure I had a visa.

"Come back tomorrow, please. Next person in line!"

TWO DAYS BEFORE my anticipated departure and the day my sister was due to leave London, I received an email from my relative Rafi telling me of a "serious mishap."

"The whole family is in such a state of mourning and mentally upset no one would be able to look after you if you come at this stage. I therefore humbly request you to cancel your tour. Since our Indian guests will also not be coming now, there will be no one to take you to Amritsar. The circumstances demand that the visit be deferred. I feel extremely sorry about all the planning and efforts you put in for this visit and the excitement that you had, but one cannot challenge the acts of nature."

Further emails trickled in. A member of the groom's party had died suddenly. Custom dictated forty days of mourning. The young people had practiced their dancing for months and the first wave of international guests had already arrived, but now flowers, food, wedding venues, hotel rooms, and club lodgings all had to be cancelled.

"It feels destined not to be," I wrote to my sister, dismayed.

"At least we are okay, alive and well!" she replied. She stayed in London. I rearranged my flight to travel directly to Delhi and then on to Amritsar alone. But there was a riot in Delhi and I couldn't shake the feeling that this journey was not to be taken. I changed my flight again and instead visited my mother in New Zealand—another trembling, mountainous land situated on tectonic fault lines. This time, the Shaky Isles felt calm and stable, and my mother felt like home.

I HAVE MY visas, one to India, the homeland of a grandfather I never knew, the other to Pakistan, home of other branches of the family tree. Like the two countries, they lie across a divide, twinned on adjoining pages in my passport.

I possess a new stone heart, a consolation prize my youngest son bought at Ten Thousand Villages, a local fair trade store. The size of my palm, it is translucent rose salt stone, halite, from a Pakistani mine in the Himalayas, equidistant from Amritsar and Lahore. It sits on my windowsill.

THE ROAR OF DISTANCE

AT FIRST, I thought the greatest distance I have known is 11,387.16 miles, or 18,325.35 kilometers, the arc flown in twenty-six hours and fifty-five minutes by an Air New Zealand plane from Auckland to London, where I used to live. Now that I live in the United States, I translate my horizons to miles; for most of my life, I calculated in metric. At times I clutch and fail to find an equivalent to miles, Fahrenheit, ounces, or pounds. I need to check in my tattered *Sure to Rise* cookbook that a softened rectangle of butter is a two-tablespoon equivalent to twenty-five grams, before it oozes out of its slimy parchment paper. Distance is like a concertina, expanding and contracting according to the quietness of the hour, strength of attachment, duration of absence, vividness of memory.

FOR THREE DELIGHTFUL years I spent weekends strolling past the ducks in St. James Park, along the Serpentine, along the South Bank of the Thames, in and out of the second-hand book stores at Charing Cross, and among the market stalls of Brixton and Notting Hill.

But over time London's pearly light tarnished in favor of the memory of another: "New Zealand light—intense, clear, particularizing, ruthless . . . it brought all things factually to stand in the light, and that's where finally one wants to see them," as Robert Creely describes it. I craved clarity—where did I belong? Should I build a life in London and sever the cord to home, to volcanoes and primal forests, to sharp, blue light, to walks along the ocean, garden walks with my mother, comfortable half-ended sentences with old friends?

The metrological visibility index measures contrasts over distance. I measure contrast over distance, and sometimes my method is faulty. Scientists say that in New Zealand, the visibility index and optical depth are immense, because of clean maritime air and high levels of ultraviolet, a part of the electromagnetic spectrum. I imagine, but cannot see. As magnetic force or myth sends the water whirling down a drain in the opposite direction, so I spun back to the Southern Hemisphere, to my homeland.

THEN I CAME to think that the greater distance I have known is that between Chicago and my mother. She sleeps restlessly seventeen hours into the future while I type at my desk during her morning of the day before. This makes little sense as I write it, and less sense when I imagine a date line coring the globe into chunks of time. I say restless, because I know she tosses and wakes often at three a.m. to the sound of the ocean heaving onto the shore near her brick duplex in Falla Street, Paraparaumu Beach, in the North Island of New Zealand, in that part of the world called AsiaPacific, Polynesia, Australasia, or

Oceania, depending on whether a geographer, anthropologist, share broker, or oceanographer is naming it. The breakers that my mother hears at three a.m. disperse all the way from Chile, 5309.57 miles, or 8544.92 kilometers, from Chicago, across the South Pacific.

This is bad science, because only tsunamis would travel that far, and she actually lives on the Tasman Sea, but I like the idea of the waves rolling toward her, beginning on a land mass connected to mine. I read that the length is calculated as:

$$L = \frac{g}{2p} \text{ T 2 or L} = 1.56 \text{ m/sec2 T 2.}$$

IN DEEP WATER, the wavelength is equal to the earth's acceleration due to gravity (g) divided by 2p times the square of the wave period (T). I don't understand. My forehead constricts when I try to imagine waves of water, sound, or light as formulas.

The value of earth's gravity, g, is 9.81 m/sec2. This equation, when combined with the general wave speed equation C = L/T, is used to determine wave speed (C) from either wavelength (L) only or wave period (T) only:

$$C = \frac{L}{T} = \frac{g\ T}{2p} \text{ or } C2 = \frac{L2}{T2} = \frac{g\ L}{2p}$$
$$C = 1.56 \text{ T or C } 2 = 1.56 \text{ L.}$$

I was never good at math, although my eldest son is, and I think of him, three and half hours away, and my mother, who may have just now switched on her bedside lamp to clarify her vagabond thoughts, as I wake to freight cars hauling coal across the great plains and a loud speaker alerting commuters that "an inbound train toward the Loop will be approaching shortly."

There are 8349.83 miles, or 13,437 kilometers, between my mother and me, or a journey in two taxis, on three planes, on a ferry and a bus, and finally, a short walk from the bus stop to her door. The journey is equal to thirty hours of sweaty sneakers removed three times for security, two in-flight romantic comedies, one in-flight dinner of fried rice and chicken medallions, one lost pair of headphones wedged somewhere between the seats. It is equal to a small roller bag of clothing in doesn't-show-the-dirt-black. Sweater, merino, v-neck. Jeans, denim, boot-cut. Five t-shirts, cotton, v-neck, rolled tightly. Mid-thigh dress with v-neck, missing eyelet above the zipper. Seven pairs of lace-trimmed underwear, two matching bras. Calfskin jacket, frayed lining. Three scarves: one pink pashmina edged in glass beads, one blue floral cotton, one red silk. A red necklace with multiple strands. Silver earrings, gold earrings. A batik sarong.

My mother complains that I wear too much black when I visit, but black withstands the miles, hours, crossed time zones, and long delays. Roses on a scarf can hide the wilting, the sudden jilt of dislocation, of being away from the family I've made, and back to my family of origin.

The distance is equal to an overnight stay with my

sister, Fliss. If I am in her house on a hill fifty concrete steps above Karaka Bay, I can see wind-tossed Wellington Harbor, usually flecked with white caps. I watch the ferry heading to Cook Strait and the South Island. Winds from all directions meet in the Strait, making the crossing treacherous for yachts and ships. When I was a kid, fifty-three people died after the interisland ferry Wahine sheared open its hull on Barrett's Reef near the harbor entrance. The recollection is my equivalent of someone else's "I remember what I was doing when President Kennedy/Martin Luther King/John Lennon was shot or men first walked on the moon." I remember a dark, rolling storm, in fact two storms crashing together over the capital city. I remember the news images of the ship on its side, not far from land. I remember the numb survivors in lifejackets stumbling to shore through mist and freezing spume.

The flat part of the peninsula is also known as Te Tūranganui-o-Kupe, because Polynesian explorer Kupe was the first person in Māori tradition to visit there. I don't know quite what he was doing there, but an outcrop is named Te Ure-o-Kupe, or "Kupe's penis," or Steeple Rock. It was changed in 2009 to Te Aroaro-o-Kupe, "Kupe's front," a more innocuous name. This is where the Wahine finally foundered after drifting up the harbor for hours. Across the harbor lies the long spine of the Rimutaka mountain range, bisecting the lower part of the North Island. Images of Wahine survivors show them staggering onto slick, jagged stones on this side of the harbor. Others perished when their lifeboats or bodies were splintered onto the rocky volcanic coast. It is hard to imagine, on days when the harbor is glassy and the ferry glides effortlessly across the surface, like a ship inside a novelty pen, floating back and forth when you tilt it, forever safe.

Through the open window at my sister's house, I hear the tug and pull of harbor water scouring small rocks back and forth, swishing me to sleep. Whenever I have trouble sleeping, I conjure this sound to lull me. Wellington was my first adult home, although I don't really think of it as being home. I lived there after I finished university, and twice subsequently. I have been visiting my sister there since she first left home as a teenager.

Several homes, and all of them different. Chicago, where I live. Auckland, where my children were born. New Plymouth, where I was born. We don't have words to capture all these nuances in English. The inadequacy marks a distance between cultures, between the British-derived culture and the indigenous Māori, who have numerous words denoting the house where you live, one's true home, one's ancestral home. Traditionally, if asked where one is from, the response places the speaker in a tribal homeland that includes the name of their ancestral canoe, their mountain, river, tribe, clan, family, chief, and marae (meeting area).

I meant to say the distance is broken by an overnight stay, but after being away for so long, my sister and I have a hollowed-out wind tunnel between us. Messages are displaced and communication misinterpreted, and the only time she visited me in the United States we argued, as we had never done. We argued about my son going to college and the possibility of him failing. Americans tend not to let fear of failure stop them from trying something, whereas New Zealanders like a concept fully built before they risk investing in it. I realized I had become quite American, or some global mash-up of cultural values from places I had lived, worked, or visited. What would have played out over many casual conversations if we had been in close proximity was compressed into one dinner-time conversation full of words tumbling out the wrong way. Neither of asked, "Why did you leave me?" or "Why have you taken so long to visit?" Neither of us said, "I resent looking after our mother," or "I feel angry that your husband took you far away from me." Instead, we hissed, "You're just like Mother," an insult that we should never shake out of its box. Once out, the space between us became five months of almost silence, punctured by occasional emails and stubbornness. For a time, that felt like the greatest distance.

As long as the journey to my sister and my mother may sound, the return journey seems at once longer, because it takes me away from them, and shorter, because it takes me back to my two sons and husband. It's possible to summon the memory of their boy-man hair and back-of-neck scents, but the real smell and curled-up proximity is so much sweeter.

A WIDE DISTANCE opened between my husband and me not long after we moved to the United States in 2001. He had taken a work contract for three years, but three months after we arrived, he told friends that he wanted to stay and not return home. We worked at our computers in the evenings, four feet between us. In bed at night, I rolled to my side and the sheets stayed cool in the twenty-four inches between us. It took many days to resume our closeness, but one morning, I woke to find the gap closed and my wrist circled by his thumb and forefinger. Now, we rarely fight, but I still have twinges of longing to be near a nikau palm with tui singing, the South Pacific foaming at my feet.

IN MY MIND'S eye, I rarely see the winter rains that blow across the isthmus horizontally from two directions, the South Pacific and the Tasman Sea, because the nostalgic memory is selective. I don't choose to recall the red tail lights snaking through rain in Auckland city gridlock, or standing cold on the rugby sidelines watching boys sloughing through mud, or bores in the drinking barns talking rugby. But if the past is the country from which I migrated, the past is now distant enough for the rose to be yellowing at the edges. I can recall what irritated me when I lived there, the unavoidable worship of rugby, phrases like "punching beyond our weight" and "world class," men entering supermarkets with bare feet and no shirts, drinking as a national sport, people who say "she'll be right." The distance between my old culture and my adopted culture expands the longer I live away from my homeland.

IN THE TIME I have been writing, I have taken a phone call from a relative, Rafi, whom I have never met. He is visiting Toronto, which is 451 miles, or 701 kilometers, away, an hour's flight. This is considerably less than the 7268.6 miles, 11,697.8 kilometers, between his home in Lahore and mine in Chicago, which makes it easier to arrange to meet each other soon, the first time I will have met someone from the Indian/Pakistani side of my family. This is further than the thirty-one miles, or fifty kilometers, that some of Rafi's family fled when India broke apart in 1947. It's a small geographic distance, but also a lifetime for the million people who were clubbed, stabbed, slashed, drowned, and shot to death, and what may have seemed like more than a lifetime to the twelve million displaced people watching the canals seep rose pink and the trains and bullock carts stain scarlet with the blood of their loved ones.

In the tangled banyan that is our family tree, our relative-in-common, my grandfather, Rafi's uncle, was not there to witness his family's caravan from India to the new Pakistan. Many years before partition, sometime in the early 1900s, my grandfather, for reasons unknown, traveled very far, from Amritsar to New Zealand, a distance of 6,921.6 nautical miles, 7,965 miles, or 12818.8 kilometers. He sailed in a ship that took about ten weeks (today one could fly 7,970.5 miles/12,827.3 kilometers in sixteen hours and thirty minutes). Was it demand for adventure, or opportunity, or necessity, or some siren call deep inside him that launched him across the ocean while his siblings stayed, for another forty or so years under the Empire's yoke? It is this distance of two—now three—generations, that I try to bridge. My materials seem flimsy and my geometry confused. In my dreams, I am unsure if I need to measure using Euclidean space or a Minkowski distance. What is the formula for a line segment or an x/y-plane? I can't find the shortest path, and I wake up with a sense of displacement, the magnitude of which is greater than the sum of making connections.

LESSER, TODAY, IS the distance to home, which I recognize as the space fashioned inside of me. I carry my home-*land* like a series of stacking dolls within my daily routine. Each contains oceans, volcanoes, streets wriggling up hills, my mother and siblings. My ideas of nationhood and selfhood are entwined, and exist inside the olive Victorian house where I currently live in Oak Park, Illinois. Soccer cleats sprawl inside the front door and a smallish boy practices drums and dilly-dallies over homework. My husband strums guitar or reclines while watching football with our youngest son draped over him. Close.

Walking my dog on the flat, straight streets of my neighborhood, I admire the plane trees with their white-patched trunks against the wide Midwestern sky, and the colorful sunbursts, stained glass, and shingles on the Painted Ladies. Later, when I pant up a steep incline on the gym treadmill, distance diminishes. I picture the vertical hill by my sister-in-law's beach house in Oakura, New Zealand. From the crest I see a panorama of ocean and livid green rainforest. That beach is my son's spiritual home, his happy place. To his bedroom wall, he pinned a photograph taken from the top of that hill. He sends me a text message with a black and white pen drawing attached—a sweep of holiday houses, cabbage palms, a half-moon bay, rocks, the Pacific Ocean that links our home islands to our current continent. Far, but not so far.

A recently emptied room echoes at the top of the stairs. My first-born left. He didn't go far in geographic terms—198 miles, or 319 kilometers, to college in Galesburg. An ocean of swaying cornfields or a three and a half hour car ride away from me, it is far enough to be absent. Distant enough that I understand my mother, who worries if there is a tornado in Oklahoma or a forest fire in California, because proximity is relative when mapped on a television screen.

The distance between my son and me expands. Wrestling practice. A heavy fall on his head. E.R. CT scan. Traumatic brain injury. On that day, those 198 miles, his twenty text messages and three phone calls seem vast—a rolling expanse between us. Hours and minutes no longer work to calculate time.

In my son's brain, at a microscopic level where the CT scan cannot penetrate, impulses scoot along his nerve fibers, his axons, from the center of his neurons. This geography contains terms that are at once familiar and strange: axon hillocks, sodium channels, branches of telo-dendria, Nodes of Ranvier. I imagine a landscape delicate and wondrous, like the lands illustrated by Dr. Seuss, or the Great Barrier Reef. Impulses light up like fireflies, dart along candy-colored neural pathways through waving fingers of coral polyps and winding streams of pink fluid, until they're interrupted. I hope my son's guidepost cells repair what's damaged, so that all of his impulses are free to travel again.

Distance loops and knots—molecular, generational, global, imagined, remembered, in waves, in gaps, imperfectly. To connect seems impossible and marvelous. I have known distances—between my beloved and me, my family and me, my homeland and here, but these seem inconsequential now. I can say, at this moment, distance lies in the limits of my language to measure the grid, to map between the markers, to keep my mind on anything while I wait for news of my boy. By far, the greatest distance I have known is between this mother and her son.

MOTH TRAP

A SEPIA PHOTOGRAPH: a Himalayan peak, a stubby fan palm. You: a young girl with black eyes, dark hair bobbed like a flapper. You wear a silk cape embroidered with gold. Your hat, in a style known as a Gandhi or Nehru cap, lurches awkwardly towards your brow. Your clothes are foreign to me, so unlike the mini skirts and knee-high boots you wore when I was small. I barely see the *you* I know, my ferocious mother, in this hesitant little bird with alien plumage.

You were among strangers. Who were they? You remember an ayah, standing in for a mother. I imagine your ayah reading you Winnie the Pooh, the adults around you dancing to "Minnie the Moocher" and "Mood Indigo." A father out of jail, a mother and baby sister dead, an almost-stepmother beginning her torment. Is that why your eyes are so wide and dark? Was it this lonely Indian sojourn that terrorized you after you returned home, keeping you bound tightly to your South Pacific birthplace?

Years later, did you pass your fear to me?

I HAVE NOT journeyed to that place, although I have journeyed to many places. I have filled up several passports, stamped Belgium, Canada, Cook Islands, Greece,

Portugal, Mexico, Samoa, Thailand, and Yugoslavia. There are multiple entries to Australia, France, Germany, Italy, Netherlands, New Zealand, Singapore, Spain, the United Kingdom, the United States. But there is no stamp for India, the cradle of my grandfather.

My long lost cousin Rafi, the son of my grandfather's sister, who trapped us down years ago (and here I meant to say "tracked" my family down. What stickiness am I afraid of, a familial moth trap?), has invited me many times to visit him in Lahore, Pakistan. His family crossed the border from Amritsar after India was splintered, after my mother's father died and family contact was lost or spurned.

When Rafi first sought out our family a lifetime later, I was living in London, a mere eight-hour flight away from him. I could have traveled there. Instead, I moved back to New Zealand, fifteen hours away, too far. Then to Chicago, thirteen hours, still too far, too dangerous. When Rafi visited Toronto a few years ago. I planned to drive to see him from Chicago, but I discovered a day earlier my passport had expired. I had let it.

I can no longer get away. Rafi, an ex-Army man and a former cricketeer, is fit and well, but is now in his eighties. He writes to me of kite flying contests in spring and eating baskets of mangos in summer. He writes that he *loves* girls. He prayed for a daughter and when she was born, he celebrated with candy, sweet meats, and music in the hospital, unlike other Pakistani families for whom daughters

inspire mourning. I want to meet this man who address-
es me as his dear daughter, who writes to tell me that he
accepts me "as a sweet real daughter, and not 'another
daughter,' because this phrase means someone 'extra.'"
He writes, "From now onwards you are not an outsider
but an intrinsic member of the family."

I think of my mother, sleepless in the dark, peering
at the southern stars as the globe spins toward her dawn.
She'll be listening to the distant wash of sea on driftwood
and pebbles, waiting for the first birds to trill from her
roses and lilies. I want her with me, to be anointed in belonging, to soothe her fault lines.

I intend to close the loop this time and visit Rafi
when he visits his sister in Toronto again. I start preparing weeks ahead, although I don't have a date. I stack up
books next to my bed, in my office, and across the dining
table. They reproach me every time I go to bed with my
iPad, or a different book, a newspaper, a cup of tea, or my
husband. If they were opened, maybe they could help. Instead, I rack up library fines before I get to them: *India: A
Portrait*, *In Light of India*, *India an Illustrated History*, *India
and Pakistan*, *Old Lahore*. I am unclear what I want from
them. I am uncertain about *Rewriting Indian History* and
Mughal India: Studies in Polity, Ideas, Society, and Culture,
but I renew them for another two weeks, and don't open
them. I am uncertain about *In Light of India* by the Mex-
ican poet and ambassador Octavio Paz, translated from
the Spanish by Eliot Weinberger. I remind myself that po-

ets so often get to the heart of the knowing, and the back cover says it is "elegant, pensive, intimate, and erudite." I need intimacy, thoughtfulness, a getting-to-the-heart of what I grasp at, a sense of what the country *is* rather than a travelogue. Then I add *Old Lahore, Reminiscences of a Resident* to the list, and my email pings, notifying me to pick up the books I've reserved, *The Amritsar Massacre* and *The Penguin Atlas of Diasporas*.

Some of these books my husband and I already own, but our chaotic system of filing books, not under 953 as on the library shelf, but on random shelves in our living room, basement, office, spare room, bedroom floor, and attic boxes meant finding the volumes took more time than reading them.

I wander from my reading repeatedly to ransack the kitchen, distract myself from discomfort, munching dried figs, dried prunes, chèvre on bread, fifteen almonds, eight brazil nuts, two slices of organic honey, roasted ham with no preservatives, a handful of pizza-flavored goldfish snacks with plenty of preservatives, and three spoons of green tea ice cream, which tasted furry because it sat uneaten in the freezer for a year. I act as if stuffing in food could suppress my anxiety.

I feel lacking in cultural knowledge, unsure how to behave with decorum, nervous about traveling alone. For many years my family neglected our heritage, or as I came to understand, denied it. The diaspora had washed out my Indian, except for the sheen on my skin, my dark eyes, and hair. My New Zealander/Britain/American-ness was uneasy with Indian-ness or Pakistani-ness—just as my mother appears in the sepia photograph, awkward in her silk costume.

As it happens, the photograph was taken, not in India as I had thought all those years, but in the garden of her grandparents' wooden house in New Zealand. The palm was not a native palm, but appeared to flourish neverthe-less, like so many transplants.

My journey is a one-hour flight from Chicago to To-ronto, a short and simple crossing. I recall Nabokov writ-ing in *Speak, Memory* that "the finder cannot unsee once it has been seen," and I wonder what my relatives might see in me. Rafi greets me at the airport. He's a slight, smiling man with a grey mustache, a brown blazer and Irish plaid cap. He holds a welcome sign decorated with a sprig of heather. I meet his siblings, Canadian citizens, and their children. The women have dark eyes and long sleek hair and I see our similarities. Rafi draws a family tree on a sheet of blue-lined paper. He tells of when he was a stu-dent in Amritsar, my grandfather's hometown, the city my mother visited when she was tiny. It was near the end of British rule and the British police beat the students with clubs, forced them on to trains and left them in the countryside far from town. The students walked back and returned to protesting. When the subcontinent was par-titioned in 1947, and the Punjab region was awash with slaughter, the family fled across the border to Lahore, to the new nation of Pakistan. Rafi tells stories of his military days, when he patrolled disputed territory in Kashmir and traveled to Indonesia and other countries for officer training. A tough man. Of course, my grandfather knew none of this. When he died, the British still ruled India and Pakistan did not exist. We talk about my grandfather and I hear how his family regarded him as a great adventurer, like Sinbad the sailor. Rafi seems disinterested when I suggest that my grandfather was perhaps not the hero he seemed. He changes the subject.

Rafi and his siblings and I drive to Niagara through thick rain. They tease each other and tell stories about growing up. The younger brother remembers that he'd kicked his teen sisters out of his car because they annoyed him with their laughter. The girls had to walk home miles alone. "What was he thinking!" Rafi sings along to a CD of ghazals, songs in Urdu. He stops now and then to translate. They are poems of unrequited love and longing set to elegant melodies. Rafi, the retired military colonel, the hard man, is poetic and sentimental. We pose in front of the Falls, in the gray pelting wet. Our umbrella blows inside out. In our photograph, my hat is lopsided and our eyes squint into the gale. A family of almost strangers, we huddle together and smile for the record.

DISPERSAL

Summer will grow old
As will the thistle, letting
A clenched bloom unfold
— RICHARD WILBUR

CORNFLOWERS:

Love-in-the-mist, *nigella damascena*, self-sows near my hydrangeas. The spiky flowers bloom the color of cloudless skies and still seas, blue flecked with white. Their ancestors came from a packet of seeds I scattered seasons ago. They remind me of my mother's garden, close to Te Tai-o-Rehua, the Tasman Sea, margin waters of the South Pacific. English colonists grew the hardy flower in their cottage beds to remind them of home, and now I do the same. A scattering, dispersion—"diaspora," from the Greek διασπορά. It sounds like the suck of water through rock pools, sibilance on faraway shores. *Di-ass-por-ahh*, the last syllable a sigh and a backward glance to my mother's beach and her love-in-the-mist, roses, lilies, clematis, jasmine, and honeysuckle.

Some plants are adventurers turned stealthy invaders, some invisible escapees, spores wafted on transcontinental winds, others cast out on the tide, shifting about the globe. Journeyers, pilgrims, exiles, nomads, transplants—dispersed.

PALM:

Once, a decapitated head bobbed before me in a dusk tide. I watched with tight jaw and prickling neck as waves sucked it back towards the horizon, then hurled it to the shore. Rolling in a wash of spume, it turned its Cyclops eye to glare at me. In the fading grey evening, I realized that the lolling head was a coconut. It had floated from some distant Pacific atoll, preparing to germinate far from its mother tree.

For a time, the idea of being an immigrant terrified me. Taking root on a distant and ambivalent shore was not what I wanted. I called myself an expatriate because that word saved me from commitment, kept one boot planted in my homeland. It protected me from complaints about undesirable implants, the rants of politicians and talkback hosts, conversations overheard at the carwash, mutterings on the Internet.

SEEDLING:

Come summer, the air fills with maple legions helicoptering across the parkway. Dandelion parachutes drift across Oak Park's gold-pocked lawns. My border collie gets grass burrs stuck in his surrender-flag tail, as he rushes at the squirrels that uproot my parsley while burying and digging up acorns.

Our garden borders cannot be protected. I dig random seedlings from the vegetable bed. By midsummer, those I missed have grown into lanky juveniles along the garage wall. Trees and plants may look stationary, but they are fervent in their work of propagation. They disseminate far and wide.

MANGROVE:

Yellow-green pods of manawa—native mangrove—float along intertidal stretches of northern New Zealand. The propagules seek purchase on silty shores. They nestle in. Settle deep. If you paddle a kayak up a Northland river estuary, you will see where they shoot up aerial roots, olive-green periscopes poking from the mudflats. Shoals of tiny mullet flit in and out of these pneumaphores, as the mangrove offspring are called. The plants extend their territory by stealth, colonizing salt marsh. Property developers rip them out, but mangroves do good. They guard against seeping zinc and copper, host whelks and crabs, slow the waves' rub and pound. Protectors of coastal edges. Securers of margins.

The kuaka, the godwit, forages here. Every year it flies almost 18,000 miles to the northern hemisphere, without pausing to eat, drink or rest—the longest non-stop journey for any bird. A-wik, a-wik, a-wik, it cries, before setting out, as Robin Hyde wrote, "on a migration beside which the swallow's blue hither and yon is a mere stroll with wings." Young New Zealanders, too, fly north, "our youth, our best, our intelligent, brave and beautiful, must make the long migration, under a compulsion they hardly understand; or else be dissatisfied all their lives long."

OAK:

I gave my brother an American pin oak for his birthday. Circled by sheep sculptures, it grows in the centre of a field adjoining his garden in the North Island of New Zealand. Real sheep outnumber humans there, two thousand to one. My brother's tree sprouts fresh leaves in his spring, about the time my neighborhood oak leaves turn yellow, floating down to cover the sidewalk in my fall. When we were kids, my brother and I played a game matching capital cities and flags to their countries, using the large wall map that hung above my bed. That map, with its immense expanse of blue sprawling far beyond our collection of southern islands, excited me to travel. I left my homeland, but my brother stayed.

On Wabash Avenue, I run into my friend Filip, a graduate film student from Ghana. He is making a film about two African cousins who come to America. One returns, the other one stays. "Why do some go and some stay?" he asks. He wrestles with the idea. "It's too hard to confront," he says. He talks of himself, but the question is also my own.

Living in the opposite hemisphere to my mother, brother, and one sister, I'm out of sync, in season and when we talk. There's dissonance between me and those who remained. Muffed communication—a misread email or skewed conversation. It reminds me of *Letters from Wonderland*, where Lewis Carroll describes a lecture where the teacher sits at the far end of the room, a scout sits outside the door, the sub-scout sits outside the outer door, the sub-sub-scout sits halfway downstairs, and down in the yard sits the pupil, with questions and answers shouted back and forth:

Tutor: *Divide a hundred by twelve!*

Scout: *Provide wonderful bells!*

Sub-Scout: *Go ride under it yourself?*

Sub-sub-scout: *Deride the dunderheaded elf!*

Pupil (surprised): *Who do you mean?*

Sub-sub-scout: *Doings between!*

Sub-scout: *Blue is the screen!*

Scout: *Soup tureen.*

And so on.

PŌHUTUKAWA:

I try not to look over my shoulder. If I do, I see red pōhutukawa blazing along summer coasts. Number eight wire fences slice across rugged hillsides. Sheep scratch against the barbs. Tufts of their wool used to stick to my clothes when I climbed over. Months later, I'd find bits in my pocket, smelling of lanoline, soothing to touch. My mother collected strands from farm boundaries. She spun the raw fleece into yarn, softly pumping the treadle of her silver beech wheel, feeding the thread on to a wooden bobbin. Then she'd knit the thread into sweaters, smelling of sheep and fields, farm brush burn-offs, morning mist, ocean summers, and longing. I remember too, the smell of my dad's manuka-smoked fish at Christmas. Fresh snapper smoked in a little smoke shed with a tin roof. *Maa-noo-ka. Maa-noo-ka.* Liking the sound of the native wood, rolling it over my tongue.

Is this nostalgia, the sickness of clinging to a candy-sweet past? It can leave your mouth with the cloying aftertaste of gum chewed too long. What is the idea of home, really? *Topophilia*, love of place, said W.H. Auden. *Endomophilia*, love of a place and culture, said Glen Albrecht. Existential insiderness, said Edward Relph, a state of homewellness, the completeness of being immersed in culture and place. When I moved to the United States, my best friend was Magda, a Polish woman who relocated with her Dutch husband and two children. For two years, we lived a block apart and together navigated our new neighborhood. She returned to the Netherlands, then to her homeland of Poland. Now she reports a gap between her and her childhood friends—that she is forever an outsider, no matter how long she is back.

"Where is home?" I ask my youngest child, who was two years old when he moved to the United States. "New Zealand, our house here, the park, our dog." My first-born has a nuanced answer. "Home *is* wherever you are. Home *is* New Zealand. But I feel *at* home in Oak Park and at college." My husband is at home wherever he lives, immersed in whatever he is doing.

For me, home is my boys, heads touching, sleeping on our sofa in the next room. The sound of my dog's tongue rasping as he licks his belly. The scarlet cardinal I see through the kitchen window, sitting amid the crabapple berries. It's also the loamy, salt-laden air of Auckland isthmus, the pointy volcanic cone poking out of the harbor. My mother, sitting in her rose-patterned chair. Pīwakawaka fanning their tails as they dart about the native trees. Pōhutukawa's vibrant crimson flowers lighting up the cliffs during the southern Christmas. Its roots can sprout out of branches and trunks, growing through the air to clutch at crevices, meandering to find moisture, clinging to cliffs, thriving in habitats often wild and inhospitable.

APPLE:

My sons were both born at home in Auckland. A heat wave sizzled during my first pregnancy. We were prohibited from watering the garden or taking baths that summer. I made hundreds of ice cubes flavored with herbs—mint, lemon balm, lemongrass, apple mint—thinking they would cool me in labor. During the final weeks of pregnancy, I rattled the cubes from their trays, lined them up in Ziploc bags and stacked them in the freezer. When contractions began, I wanted nothing on my lips. The bags remained unopened. The first rain in months fell early the morning I gave birth, pattering lightly on the tin roof of our house. My friend Ross made a chocolate birthday cake, but I couldn't eat. He put the remains in the refrigerator. Two days later, I asked for cake. I had seen it earlier, wrapped in a white plastic bag, but the cake was all eaten. What was actually in the plastic bag was the placenta, the whenua. The midwife saved it in case we wanted to bury it in the earth according to Māori custom. My carefully arranged ice cubes left no room in the freezer, so the midwife placed the placenta on the middle shelf of the refrigerator, next to the milk. She forgot to tell us. When my sleep-deprived husband discovered it, he took a spade to the rock-hard ground. The rain had barely dampened the surface. He scraped away for an hour and buried the whenua under the apple tree. Five years later, our second son was born at dawn, in a different house, not during a drought. My husband dug into soft dirt and buried our boy's placenta under another tree. Both boys are therefore linked irrevocably to that land.

ELM:

Near my house, near a retirement home, is a four-acre woodland park full of mature trees and a prairie grass-lined path that I often walk along on my way home. One afternoon as I strolled through, an elderly woman called to me. Sitting alone on a bench in sunlight filtering through elm leaves, she said she was lonely and wanted to talk. I sat with her for a while. She migrated from Austria with her husband when she was young, and raised her children here. They were all gone now. She was the only one left. "Don't let that happen to you," she said. "Go back while you are still young and can make a life. Don't be left here."

THE MILES BETWEEN ME

I DROPPED MY firstborn in a cornfield, in a land at once foreign and familiar. My husband and I drove our son southwest to college, past grain silos and flat soybean fields, where the horizons seemed elastic and the afternoon sky unnaturally cloudless and blue. We sped across the plain in silence. I was wedged in the back seat with an ironing board digging into my hip and a heavy canvas sliding into my head. My son had his headphones on. My husband focused on the road, until a cop pulled us over and cited us for speeding, just before the off-ramp to Galesburg.

I had dreaded this time, but as it sidled closer, my resistance loosened. My son's journey was insignificant in distance, at least compared to our family's movement from New Zealand to Chicago, over a decade earlier. I could deal with an Illinois town with one traffic light in a way I could not comprehend Boston or Florida, and a great expanse of the continent between us. I was afraid of losing him out there. I could let him be American, mile by mile, but not state by state. American-ness had been seeping into him anyway. He'd switched from Marmite to peanut butter and jelly, rugby to football and wrestling, trading his All Blacks jersey for a Bears shirt, from learning the haka to singing "Take Me Out to the Ball Game." These changes blurred into my life, as water paints soak into artist's paper, embedding color into the fiber without revealing the edges.

Diaspora, dispersal, seemed inevitable by about his junior year of high school. I tried coaxing him to return to New Zealand, hoping to sew him back in there. Once, I'd said that teenagers thought they were invincible. He'd disagreed. He was afraid of guns, he said. I wanted him to be somewhere that seemed safer, where handguns and assault weapons weren't allowed. And the tuition costs were one-seventh of what we would pay here, student loans interest-free, the healthcare covered. I wanted him to have the freedom I had when I was a student—to read and hike and explore without the burden of debt. I balked at what the cost would mean for me, also. But he preferred to stay here. So there we were, joining a generation of American youth echoing their forebears' journeys across the continent, in minivans loaded with flat screen televisions and coordinated dorm room sets.

We stopped at a small Midwestern liberal arts college, famed as part of the Underground Railroad and venue for a Lincoln-Douglas debate. A hive of upperclassmen swarmed our overstuffed SUV. Into the concrete block dorm room, they whisked my son's new plaid comforter, mini-fridge, extra-long twin sheets, ramen noodles, seventy-two-count container of laundry detergent pods, liter beer glass bought in Munich, and duffel bags sausaged with forty t-shirts, ten sweatshirts, six pairs of jeans, five carefully curated pairs of shoes, and twelve caps.

We banged nails, hung, ordered, arranged, glued, and smoothed his possessions into a kind-of-homeliness. It didn't smell of our house, Murphy's oil soap, stir-fried onions, and fresh-picked hydrangeas. It didn't smell of his room in our house, a distinct mix of boy sweat, day-old Doritos, gym gear and damp towels, Armani cologne. It didn't smell of him, not yet. No, this room smelled of painted concrete, steam-cleaned carpet, cardboard, and plastic. The anonymous scent of an institution, waiting to absorb the identity of a new inhabitant.

I snuck in a hug with my boy when we were alone, my private farewell. I saw he would be okay, that I would be okay. Later, on a wide lawn between the auditorium and the bell tower, parents sobbed and wailed. In photographs, my son looks cocky, with his cap on backwards and his arm slung around my neck, only a slight tightness in his smile betraying his nerves. My throat tensed as he strode inside, away from me. Another American rite of passage was behind us.

A few months earlier, we had watched him graduate from high school. We had sweltered in the unsheltered bleachers of the football stadium as his class received their diplomas, girls in white gowns, boys in dark suits and red ties. I'd watched him play football in this stadium, among cheerleaders and the school marching band.

I'd watched these events as a cultural outsider, absorbing the iconography and slowly making it my own.

There had always been four of us. Now we were down to three. How would it be, without that one, the one who taught us to be parents, who taught us to be a family, who led me through the traditions and routines of school, sports, and community life in America? Who taught me to say water as a Chicagoan, "waa-derr," when a waiter did not understood my Kiwi "wah-tah." Who helped me trade rugby for football and baseball, and introduced me to urban youth culture—low-rider pants, complicated fist bumps, and the acronym for "you only live once."

THERE IS, AS Annie Dillard observes, a "kind of seeing that involves a letting go."

My husband and I drove back through the fields, all bronze now with the sun low. I noticed, really noticed, the remains of the prairie beauty: blazing goldenrod, the last of the coppery corn dying back, yellow grasses—a dramatic shift from the ocean blues and deep greens of my homeland. Now I appreciated the muted splendor of the cornfields, nothing flashy or overly dramatic, just a quiet goldenness laid out between the horizons, offering itself to me if I paid close enough attention. The Midwestern plain.

We drove back, we two, back to our one, with the setting sun huge and alight and magnificent in the rear-view mirror. My son was back there. I texted him, asking him to look at the big red sun. He texted straight back, "you mean *orange* sun?" A joke about our inability to agree on colors. Then the road dipped, the sun vanished. We carved back through the darkness to the home that felt a little less like home, and opened the door of the empty bedroom. My younger son opened the closet, removed a sweatshirt, and lay on his brother's bed clutching it against his face, sucking in its smell.

Boy-gone quiet reigns in our house. It is the first thing I notice. It is the rest of my life.

ACKNOWLEDGMENTS

Thanks to the journals where versions of the following essays first appeared: "The Rights and Privileges of an Alien" and "Unraveling" in *Guernica*, "Meditations on Brown" in *The Offing*, "A Regret" published as "The Palace of Regret" in *The Prague Revue*, and "The Displeasure of the Table" in *The Rumpus*. I'm grateful to *The Rumpus* for nominating my work for a Pushcart Prize.

It was a privilege to work with Curbside Splendor Publishing. Thanks to my wonderful editors Naomi Hoffman and Catherine Eves who shepherded this work with grace and care, Alban Fischer for a beautiful design, and Victor David Giron.

Thanks to David Lazar, Aviya Kushner, Jenny Boully, Garnett Kilberg-Cohen, Ken Daley, Mehrnaz Saeedafa, Albert Laguna, Sam Weller and Ruth Leitman for direction and mentorship. I am grateful to have received a Follet Fellowship from Columbia College Chicago.

Kate Burns, José Orduña, Kristen Ratke, Colleen O'Connor, Tatiana Uhoch, Wes Jamieson, Micah O'Crary, Ryan

Spooner, Sharon Burns, Jennifer Tatum and Ali Carpenter—thanks for giving good workshop.

My writer friends in Chicago and beyond, thank you for your generosity and support. David MacLean, Peggy Shinner, and Megan Stielstra, I am humbled. The Marrow, the Guild, Wit Rabbit, and the 33 Series. Hillary Brenhouse, Martha Bayne, Zoe Zolbrod, Darcy Cosper. Robert Labate. Magda, Amy, Angela, Liz, Dipika, Nic, Deepak and Vivek, my First Friday friends and Oak Park Acorns, thanks for reading essays along the way.

I am indebted to my family. To my mother, for courage, fortitude and sharing a love of nature. My siblings and nieces and nephews in Aotearoa, the U.K. Germany and Australia, you are never far away. Rafi, I am so grateful you tracked us down and closed the circle. My Toronto family, thank you for your hospitality and warmth.

Special thanks to Bruce—never and always. Arlo and Leroy, my cup overflows. Thanks for your patience, stories and so much fun.

TONI NEALIE is a writer, journalist, and teacher living in Chicago. Her work has appeared in *Guernica*, *The Prague Review*, *The Offing*, *The Rumpus*, and been nominated for a Pushcart Prize. She worked in magazines, politics, and public relations in the U.K and her native New Zealand before moving to the U.S.—two weeks before 9/11. She holds an MFA from Columbia College Chicago.

Curbside ✺ *Splendor*

CHICAGO INDEPENDENT PUBLISHING

"With this voice-driven novel,
Dave Reidy moves into the front ranks
of Chicago writers."

—DAVID LEAVITT,
AUTHOR OF *THE TWO HOTEL FRANCFORTS*

curbsidesplendor.com ◼ CurbsideSplendorPublishing 🐦 CurbsidePress

Curbside  Splendor

CHICAGO INDEPENDENT PUBLISHING

"Half romance, half meditation on global affairs, *Juventud* portrays how the past can affect the present and how memory can be fallible."

—FOREWORD REVIEWS

curbsidesplendor.com   CurbsideSplendorPublishing   CurbsidePress

Curbside 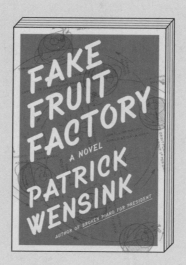 Splendor

CHICAGO INDEPENDENT PUBLISHING

"A comedy machine pumping out madcap action, large-scale disaster, and one strange character after another. Also, fake fruit."

—OWEN KING,
AUTHOR OF *DOUBLE FEATURE*

curbsidesplendor.com   CurbsideSplendorPublishing   CurbsidePress

Curbside 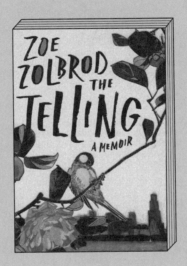 *Splendor*

CHICAGO INDEPENDENT PUBLISHING

"A gripping read. *The Telling* is brutally honest, relentlessly passionate, and ferociously intelligent."

—ROB ROBERGE,
AUTHOR OF *LIAR* AND *THE COST OF LIVING*

curbsidesplendor.com CurbsideSplendorPublishing CurbsidePress